THE CUSTOMARY PRACTICE OF HEADCOVERINGS

THE CUSTOMARY PRACTICE OF HEADCOVERINGS

AN EXEGETICAL/HISTORICAL STUDY OF 1 CORINTHIANS 11:2-16 PRESENTED IN A SERIES OF LETTERS

Greg L. Price

Published by Gospel Covenant Publications
Lewiston, Idaho, USA

www.gcpublications.com
info@gcpublications.com

ISBN: 978-0-9828564-6-8

TABLE OF CONTENTS

INTRODUCTION

The issue of women being covered in worship or not being covered in worship is a controversy that divides and separates churches and Christians within the Visible Church. Thus, it is an issue worthy of discussion with a view to the peace, purity, and unity of Christ's Church.

The present series of letters on the subject of headcoverings occurred between the author and an officer in another Presbyterian Church by way of an informal discussion of both Scripture and history.

The author of these letters was a minister in the Reformed Presbytery in North America (RPNA) at the time that a position paper on the subject of headcoverings in worship ("The Practice Of Headcoverings In Public Worship") was adopted (June 4, 2001) by Presbytery. This position paper was written in order to repent of its former position (wherein the uncovered head of men and the covered head of women in worship were viewed as specifically regulated by Scripture per the Regulative Principle of Worship) and in order to clarify its present position, that the uncovered head of men and the covered head of women in worship (as taught by Paul in 1 Corinthians 11) were cultural and customary practices that are NOT specifically regulated by Scripture (per the Regulative Principle of Worship). Being cultural and customary practices, they may be altered from culture to culture, from nation to nation, and from age to age. The thrust of the position paper ("The Practice Of Headcoverings In Public Worship") was more of a historical than an exegetical presentation, which on that account has led

7

some to dismiss the position adopted by the RPNA.

In the present series of letters on the subject of headcoverings, there has been a concerted effort made to demonstrate that not only a historical evaluation, but most importantly, an exegetical evaluation of Paul's inspired words in his letter of 1 Corinthians (Chapter 11, Verses 2-16) leads to the same conclusion arrived by the Reformed Presbytery in North America (RPNA) in its position paper ("The Practice Of Headcoverings In Public Worship"). The goal in this charitable exchange of letters was not debate (for debate's sake), but rather an earnest desire to strive for unity and uniformity in the truth of Jesus Christ. Likewise, the goal in making these letters public (which was also endorsed by the officer of the Presbyterian Church with whom the exchange occurred) is to endeavor a charitable presentation and testimony of the exegetical and historical reasons for the cultural and customary view of the uncovered head of men and covered head of women in worship from an analysis of 1 Corinthians 11:2-16.

There has been some slight editing of the original letters to correct spelling, punctuation, grammar, and in a few cases to fill out and clarify the meaning of a sentence or phrase. Also, all names and personal information have been edited out of these letters. An attempt to spell Greek words in English letters was made, but not having the proper font has placed limitations on the spelling of Greek words. The officer in the Presbyterian Church with whom the exchange occurred is simply designated by an underlined space (e.g. ___). It is my earnest desire and prayer that the Lord may promote the unity and uniformity of His Church by means of these letters. My praise is offered to the Lord for this opportunity and thanks to the brother with whom the discussion in these letters transpired.

Greg L. Price (August 2011)

Letters Responding to Argument #1 (1 Corinthians 11:2) and the Position of the Westminster Standards

February 4, 2011

Dear _____,

Thank you once again for allowing me an opportunity to respond to the main points of your position on women being veiled in worship (as required by the regulative principle of worship). I will not respond to each of your 8 arguments all at one time in this first installment, but will break them down to responding to one or two of your arguments at a time in subsequent installments. In so doing, I can get a response back to you more quickly (even if it is not complete), and you may take the opportunity to reply to a more brief response from me rather than having to reply to a more extensive response from me. I hope this facilitates more interaction between us on specific arguments rather than treating them in a cursory manner. I would like to address in this first installment some historical testimony (particularly the Westminster Standards), and then address your first argument from 1 Corinthians 11:2.

HISTORICAL TESTIMONY – THE WESTMINSTER STANDARDS

At the outset, as I indicated in a previous email, I believe the divines of the First and Second Reformations spoke with one voice that the veiling of women in view here in 1 Corinthians 11 did not fall under the category of "the regulative principle of worship", but rather was an outward customary sign among the culture of the Corinthians (as in other locations of the ancient world). Yes, behind that customary sign for women (and the lack of it for men) were revealed moral principles that were unalterable and always to be observed (in every age and culture) in regard to submission, authority, proper gender distinctions, and proper decorum in worship. But that is quite different from saying that the customary sign itself is unalterable. ____, if you have found any divines of the First or Second Reformations that state that the covered head (or the lack of it) was not a customary sign in worship (but rather a moral or regulative principle sign for all ages and nations), I would appreciate knowing of any such divines. I realize that we cannot rest our case on the universal agreement of the divines of the First and Second Reformations (our case must rest on Scripture); however, I have come over the years to appreciate the collective wisdom and amazing discernment granted to these extraordinary men, especially when they speak with one voice in unanimity.

In regard to this historical testimony, I would also state that in the Westminster Subordinate Standards the matter of covering the head for women in worship (or the uncovering of the head for men in worship) does not occur even once under the category of regulated worship (i.e. regulated according to the commandment of

God) either in the *Confession of Faith*, in the *Directory For The Public Worship of God*, or in the *Form of Presbyterial Church Government*. It should seem strange to any of us who know how careful these divines were in articulating what was *required* to be used in worship that they omitted this matter altogether (if it is specifically regulated by Scripture). Can you think of any other element or part of worship (that is clearly authorized by God in His Word) that was entirely omitted from the *Confession of Faith*, the *Directory For The Public Worship of God*, or the *Form of Presbyterial Church Government*? I cannot think of one. The scripturally regulated use of covering for women (and non-covering for men) escapes mention altogether by the Westminster divines in the *Confession of Faith* in the list given of regulated elements and parts of worship:

> Prayer, with thanksgiving, being one special part of religious worship, is by God required of all men (21:3).

> The reading of the Scriptures with godly fear; the sound preaching, and conscionable hearing of the word, in obedience unto God, with understanding, faith, and reverence; singing of psalms with grace in the heart; as also the due administration and worthy receiving of the sacraments instituted by Christ; are all parts of the ordinary religious worship of God: besides religious oaths and vows, solemn fastings, and thanksgivings upon special occasions, which are, in their several times and seasons, to be used in an holy and religious manner (21:5).

Likewise the scripturally regulated use of covering for

women (and non-covering for men) escapes mention altogether by the Westminster divines in the *Directory For The Public Worship of God*. Certainly in this document on worship that lists and describes the various ordinances that are regulated by God's Word, one would expect to find the covering of women (and the uncovering of men), if it was a scripturally regulated act of worship. However, as we consider the list of regulated ordinances that fall under the category of "Public Worship" (which are found as various headings within the *Directory For The Public Worship of God*), we find the following regulated ordinances mentioned: the Reading of the Holy Scripture, Public Prayer, the Preaching of the Word, the Sacraments, Days of Fasting and Thanksgiving, and the Singing of Psalms. But there is no mention of headcoverings.

Finally, the scripturally regulated use of covering for women (and non-covering for men) escapes mention altogether by the Westminster divines in the *Form of Presbyterial Church Government*. There is a list of scripturally regulated ordinances for a church found in the *Form of Presbyterial Church Government* under the heading, "Of the Ordinances in a particular Congregation":

> The ordinances in a single congregation are, prayer, thanksgiving, and singing of psalms, the word read, (although there follow no immediate explication of what is read,) the word expounded and applied, catechising, the sacraments administered, collection made for the poor, dismissing the people with a blessing.

But once again, there is absolute silence in regard to the use of headcoverings in worship. How did the Westminster divines miss this in all of their various statements regarding worship if indeed they believed that the veiling of women in worship and the non-veiling of men in worship were scripturally regulated acts or parts of worship? ___, if you can give some explanation why you believe the Westminster divines omitted any mention of headcoverings as a scripturally regulated act of worship, I would appreciate your thoughts. Surely, there must be a reason if the veiling of women in worship and the non-veiling of men in worship was a Divine ordinance specifically regulated by Scripture.

Although nothing at all is mentioned in the text of the *Confession of Faith*, the *Directory For The Public Worship of God*, or the *Form of Presbyterial Church Government* about the veiling of women in worship (or the non-veiling of men in worship), let alone it being a scripturally regulated practice in worship that is morally and perpetually required by God in His Word, when we consider the proof texts used by the Westminster divines, we find that 1 Corinthians 11:13,14 was used as a proof text in the *Confession of Faith* (1:6):

> The whole counsel of God, concerning all things necessary for his own glory, man's salvation, faith, and life, is either expressly set down in scripture, or by good and necessary consequence may be deduced from scripture: unto which nothing at any time is to be added, whether by new revelations of the Spirit, or traditions of men. Nevertheless, we acknowledge the inward illumination of the Spirit of God to be necessary for the saving understanding of such things as are revealed in the word; and that there are some circumstances concerning the worship of God, and government of the

14

Church, common to human actions and societies, which are to be ordered by the light of nature and Christian prudence, according to the general rules of the word, which are always to be observed.

If I may briefly expound on three points in this portion of our *Confession of Faith* (to which we both subscribe).

First, the placement of this proof text (as found in 1 Corinthians 11:13,14) and what it supports in the text is significant. For it is not provided as a proof text for any truths stated in the entire first sentence. In the first sentence, it is stated that, "The whole counsel of God, concerning all things necessary for his own glory, man's salvation, faith, and life . . . ;" and this would certainly include any ordinance of worship that is specifically regulated by Scripture. For worship of the Triune God clearly is necessary to "his own glory", "man's salvation", and "faith"; and every ordinance of worship that is specifically regulated by Scripture MUST BE "either expressly set down in scripture, or by good and necessary consequence may be deduced from scripture." Thus, if the veiling of women in worship and the unveiling of men in worship is specifically governed by the Regulative Principle of Worship or by the Moral Law of God, they must be comprehended under this first sentence in the *Confession of Faith* (1:6).

Second, there is a clear contrast that begins with the second sentence (as indicated by the word, "Nevertheless"). While the objective testimony of Scripture is sufficient for all things necessary to God's glory, man's salvation, and all matters of faith (including worship that is regulated expressly or deductively by God's Word), there is also the subjective, inward illumination of the Holy Spirit that is necessary for the "saving understanding" of all things objectively set forth in Scripture. Then after the semi-colon (;) in the second sentence, there appears the connective ("and"), which indicates that what follows is also a part of the contrast to the first sentence (i.e. what is said after the semi-colon is also part of the contrast that begins with "Nevertheless"): "**AND** that there are some circumstances concerning the worship of God, and government of the Church, common to human actions and societies, which are to be ordered by the light of nature and Christian prudence, according to the general rules of the word, which are always to be observed" (emphasis added).

Third, that which is here distinguished in the second sentence after the semi-colon (;) is that which is NOT expressly or deductively set down in Scripture from that in the first sentence which IS expressly or deductively set down in Scripture. After the semi-colon (;), the divines begin to deal with "some circumstances CONCERNING the worship of God [not *in sacra,* i.e. "in worship"; but *circa sacra,* i.e. "concerning worship" – GLP], and government of the Church, COMMON TO HUMAN ACTIONS AND SOCIETIES." This is the place where the Westminster divines chose to place the proof text concerning headcoverings as found in 1 Corinthians 11:13,14. Why didn't they place that proof text in the first sentence where all scripturally regulated worship must be included? Why did they place that proof text in the second sentence (which addresses "some circumstances concerning the worship of God, and government of the Church, COMMON TO HUMAN ACTIONS AND SOCIETIES") instead of in the first sentence (where all ordinances of scripturally regulated worship would surely occur)? My brother, I submit it was because the Assembly of divines did not believe that the veiling of women (or the non-veiling of men) was an ordinance of worship governed by the Regulative Principle of Worship. To the contrary, they believed the veiling of women (and the non-veiling of men) fell into the category of "circumstances common to human actions and societies" (which circumstances indeed vary from culture to culture, from age to age, and from nation to nation). These circumstances common to human actions and societies are NOT regulated by Scripture (either expressly or inferentially), but are to be ordered by the "light of nature", "Christian prudence", and the "general rules of the word". Because the veiling of women (and the non-veiling of men) as a common action within the society of Corinth (in distinguishing the respective roles of men and women) was agreeable to the Light of Nature, the veiling of women (and the non-veiling of men) in worship ought not to be cast aside when they engaged in the public worship of God. In other words, it is BECAUSE the veiling of women (and non-veiling of men) was practiced as a human action common to the society of Corinth (and because the practice was agreeable to the Light of Nature, which teaches the headship of men and the submission of women) that women were not to remove their headcovering when they entered the Church to worship and that men were not to cover their heads when they entered the Church to worship. Both women and men were to use the same customary signs in worship that were used in human society at large.

Moreover, the actual statements of commissioners to the Westminster Assembly (as well as the practice of the faithful Church of Scotland in her purest times) confirm this is the proper interpretation of this section of the *Confession of Faith* and its proof texts.

George Gillespie

Gillespie discusses three kinds of signs: natural, customary, and voluntary. He places headcoverings among the customary signs.

There are three sorts of signs here to be distinguished. 1. Natural signs: so smoke is a sign of fire, and the dawning of the day a sign of the rising of the sun. 2. **Customable signs; and so the uncovering of the head, which of old was a sign of preeminence, has, through custom, become a sign of subjection.** 3. Voluntary signs, which are called *signa instituta* [*instituted signs*]; these are either sacred or civil. To appoint sacred signs of heavenly mysteries or spiritual graces is God's own peculiar [prerogative], and of this kind are the holy sacraments. Civil signs for civil and moral uses may be, and are, commendably appointed by men, both in church and commonwealth; and thus the tolling of a bell is a sign given for assembling, and has the same signification both in ecclesiastical and secular assemblings. . . . Secondly, **customary signs** have likewise place in divine service; for so a man coming into one of our churches in time of public worship, if he see the hearers covered [apparently both men and women were covered in the Scottish worship service, contrary to what Paul states in 1 Corinthians 11 where a distinction is to be made between the covering of women and the non-covering of men—GLP], he knows by this **customary sign** that sermon has begun (*A Dispute Against English Popish Ceremonies*, Naphtali Press, pp. 247,248, emphases in bold is added).

Please note that Gillespie (like the Westminster Standards) distinguishes between unalterable regulated signs in worship and customary signs in worship that are subject to alteration from culture to culture, from nation to nation, and from age to age. Also note how the customary practice of the faithful Church of Scotland did NOT follow the customary practice of the Church of Corinth (as articulated by the Apostle Paul).

Samuel Rutherford

Rutherford likewise agrees with Gillespie when he states,

> The Jews to this day, as of old, used not uncovering the head as a sign of honor: But by the contrary, covering was a sign of honor. If therefore the Jews, being made a visible Church, shall receive the Lord's Supper, and pray and prophesy with covered heads, men would judge it no dishonoring of their head, or not of disrespect of the Ordinances of God. Though Paul having regard to **a national custom**, did so esteem it (*The Divine Right of Church Government and Excommunication*, Still Waters Revival Books, pp. 89,90, emphases added in bold).

Rutherford indicates that the covered head was the customary and national sign of honor to the Jews, although Paul viewed the covered head as just the opposite in Corinth.

Dear ___, I firmly believe that sufficient testimony is herein presented to indicate that neither the *Confession of*

19

Faith, nor the *Directory For The Public Worship of God,* nor the *Form of Presbyterial Church Government* (which are our Subordinate Standards) give any shred of evidence to the view that the veiling of women in worship or the non-veiling of men in worship was to be specifically regulated by Scripture (either expressly or deductively). To the contrary, the complete omission of the veiling of women in worship (and the non-veiling of men in worship), and the placing of the only proof text dealing with the veiling of women in worship within a section of the *Confession of Faith* that deals with "circumstances common to human actions and societies" indicate that our Subordinate Standards do not allow us to make the veiling of women and the non-veiling of men in worship an ordinance in worship that is regulated by Scripture (either expressly or deductively). If you know of some place in our Subordinate Standards where the veiling of women and the non-veiling of men in worship is taught and comprehended under the Regulative Principle of Worship, please identify that place (or those places). My brother, my concern at this point is that in requiring the veiling of women in worship (as being an ordinance governed by the Regulative Principle of Worship) removes us from the clear teaching of our Subordinate Standards. I would submit that any session, presbytery, synod, or general assembly that subscribes to the Westminster Standards should in all honesty take exception to the teaching of the Westminster Standards if they should require women to be covered and men to be uncovered in worship on the basis of the Regulative Principle of Worship or the Moral Law of God, for such a view is not agreeable to the Westminster Standards. But even more importantly (as I hope to demonstrate in emails that will follow), to make the covering of women and uncovering of men in worship an ordinance of worship governed by the Regulative Principle of Worship is adding a sacred sign to worship which

God has not commanded or authorized ("God alone is lord of the conscience, and hath left it free from the doctrines and commandments of men which are in any thing contrary to his word, or beside it, in matters of faith or worship" *Confession of Faith*, 20:2). Thank you for your patience in allowing me to set forward what appears to me to be the clear teaching of our Subordinate Standards.

FIRST ARGUMENT FROM 1 CORINTHIANS 11:2

___, in the remainder of this email, I would like to respond to your first scriptural argument from 1 Corinthians 11 (which you state as follows):

> Paul begins chapter 11 v. 2 by praising those who kept the ordinances, but what ordinances? I understand the ordinances he is about to speak of, which are the proper use of headcovering, the proper observance or the Lord's Supper, and proper use of spiritual gifts [from your email dated 1/20/11 – GLP].

First, Paul's praise of the Corinthian Church includes not only their remembering Paul, but also their keeping or holding to the "ordinances" as Paul delivered them to the church ("Now I praise you, brethren, that ye remember me in all things, and keep the ordinances, as I delivered them to you" 1 Corinthians 11:2). Paul is here commending them for keeping and holding to (which certainly would mean that the church was also faithfully practicing whatever "ordinances" Paul had in mind). For you can hardly be praised for keeping or holding to that which you are not practicing. For instance, would we praise our respective congregations for keeping the ordinance of psalm singing in worship, if our congregations were singing hymns in worship (or singing hymns along with psalms in worship)? Absolutely not! That is simply to say that I cannot understand from the words of Paul that he includes in the "ordinances" for which the Church of Corinth is praised, the covering of women in worship and the non-covering of men in worship. For the women (at least some significant portion of the women) were NOT covering themselves in worship, and possibly the men WERE covering themselves in worship. IF (for the sake of argument) the covering of women in worship was one of the "ordinances" in worship governed by the Regulative Principle of Worship and was one of the "ordinances" for which Paul commended them for keeping, how can Paul in the immediately following verses (1 Corinthians 11:3-16) imply that the women in the Church of Corinth were not covering themselves in worship (and therefore, not keeping the "ordinances" according to your position)? Why would Paul praise them for keeping an "ordinance" that they are not keeping (and which the Presbytery in Corinth is not keeping by tolerating the uncovering of the women in worship)? I submit that Paul has in view unnamed "ordinances" in 1 Corinthians 11:2 that were actually being faithfully kept and practiced by the Church of Corinth, and thus, the reason for his commendation and praise of the church for keeping them. Paul begins with SINCERE commendation for the church where they can be commended. I do not believe Paul is commending the church for allowing women to do what is non-commendatory (i.e. uncovering themselves in worship). Such a supposition would make the words of Paul laughable, and would evacuate of all significance what it means to actually "keep" the Divine ordinances that God has committed to us. Thus, I do not understand that Paul is calling the veiling of women an "ordinance" in 1 Corinthians 11:2.

Second, the word "ordinances" refers to the "traditions" (*paradoseis*) of the apostles. The "traditions" of the apostles were inspired, apostolic revelations received from Christ and delivered (*paradidomi*) either in the writing of Scripture or handed down by word of mouth to the church (2 Thessalonians 2:15; 2 Thessalonians 3:6). Examples of this apostolic tradition specifically identified as such in 1 Corinthians include the Lord's Supper (1 Corinthians 11:23) and the Gospel (1 Corinthians 15:3). Both Jesus and Paul abominate the "traditions" of men (Matthew 15:3,6; Galatians 1:14; Colossians 2:8), for they elevate themselves to an equal or superior authority to apostolic "traditions" received from Christ by inspiration of the Holy Spirit. If (for the sake of argument) the veiling of women (and the non-veiling of men) in worship is a "tradition", it then must be that which was directly received by the apostles through Divine revelation of the Holy Spirit. That would make the sign of the veiling of women in worship a "tradition" equal to that of the Lord's Supper and to the Gospel itself. It seems that if the veiling of women (and non-veiling of men) in worship was such an apostolic "tradition" received directly by revelation from Christ, that Paul omitted the weightiest argument in favor of a woman being covered and a man being uncovered in worship. However, the veiling of women in worship (beginning with the actual discussion of it by Paul in 1 Corinthians 11:3) is never called a "tradition" or one of the "traditions", whereas the Lord's Supper is referred to as that which was "delivered" (*paradidomi*) by way of apostolic tradition to the Church of Corinth (1 Corinthians 11:23). Thus, the only clear reference to that which was a

23

"tradition" in 1 Corinthians 11-14 is the Lord's Supper — not the veiling of women.

Third, IF (for the sake of argument) the veiling of women in worship (and the non-veiling of men in worship) was an "ordinance" or "tradition" governed by the Regulative Principle of Worship, when did it begin to be such? Nothing is stated in the Old Testament about women being required by scriptural regulation to be covered in worship (or men to be uncovered in worship). Moreover, clearly men (at least the priests) were covered in worship (Exodus 28:4,37,40), contrary to what Paul teaches in 1 Corinthians 11:4. Moreover, Jesus did not address the issue at all, nor did the other apostles do so in any of their epistles. If the veiling of women in worship and the non-veiling of men in worship is specifically regulated by Scripture, it seems odd (to say the least) that this alleged regulated "ordinance" was first introduced by Paul. Did Eve wear a headcovering as an "ordinance" commanded by God in her worship of the Lord while yet in the Garden of Eden? The Scripture states both Adam and Eve were "naked", and nothing is mentioned about a headcovering for Eve, even though the moral principles of headship and submission were clearly to be observed even in their innocent state. Thus, was this the only regulated part of worship that was introduced by Paul exclusively? All the other regulated parts of new covenant worship clearly had their origin in the Old Testament and were continued into the New Testament (such as prayer, the reading of Scripture, exposition of Scripture, psalm-singing, the benediction, the sacraments, oaths, vows, and covenants, the Sabbath). And although the outward administration of the sacraments and the Sabbath has changed, they are in essence the same as that which was instituted in the Old Testament. However, if one changes the use of the covered head so that men (at

24

least the priests, if not all men) are required to be covered in worship in the Old Testament, but required to be uncovered in the New Testament, one has altered the very essence of the meaning of the headcovering as taught by Paul (which is that to be covered is an unalterable sign of submission to the opposite gender in worship, and to be uncovered is an unalterable sign of headship to the opposite gender in worship). Is the veiling of women and the non-veiling of men in worship the only regulated act or practice in New Covenant worship that does not have its origin in the Old Testament? I do not believe the Scripture warrants such a position. However, my brother, I would be open to an explanation from you for such a unique standing of this alleged Divine "ordinance" of the covered head in worship.

Fourth, I jump ahead to 1 Corinthians 11:16 for a brief moment, where Paul infers that the veiling of a woman in worship was a "custom". For when Paul states, "we have no such custom", I take that to mean that we have no such custom of women praying unto God uncovered (1 Corinthians 11:13). Therefore, I deduce that if it was NOT a custom for women to pray uncovered, Paul infers it WAS a custom for women to pray covered. That makes Paul's remarks in 1 Corinthians 11:14,15 parenthetical. For Paul asks the following question in 1 Corinthians 11:13: "Is it comely that a woman pray unto God uncovered?" And then he answers that question in 1 Corinthians 11:16: "We have no such custom." "Custom" (sunetheia), according to Bauer, Arndt, and Gingrich is a "habit, custom, usage" (*A Greek-English Lexicon of the New Testament*, p. 797). The only other usage of this Greek word for "custom" (sunetheia) in the Received Text of the New Testament is found in John 18:39, where it refers to the "custom" of the Jews to release one prisoner at the time of the Passover (which was obviously a national

25

custom for the nation of the Jews, just as the covered head for women was a national custom among the nations and societies of the Greeks). Here Paul refers to the veiling of women as a "custom", which is precisely what the Reformers called it as well: a custom or customary sign. But a "custom" or "customary sign" is not the same thing as a scripturally regulated act or practice of worship. A "customary sign" first becomes a "custom" in the society or culture at large, and is then carried over into worship when a church is planted in that cultural society, because to dismiss such a "customary sign" in worship would introduce confusion, disorder, and schism into the church (especially when that "customary sign" is agreeable to the Light of Nature which teaches the submission of women and the headship of men in all societies and in all ages). However, when in a society, nation, or culture, there is no such general or universal custom of women covering their heads when they are in public (or for men to uncover their heads when they are in public), I submit there is no sound reason for the covering of the head in the case of women and the uncovering of the head in the case of men to be required in the public worship of God. The Corinthians are here rebuked by Paul because the women removed the customary sign of a covered head (and perhaps the men added the customary sign of a covered head) when they appeared in public worship, thus completely inverting their respective roles as outwardly indicated by the customary signs of that general society within Corinth (and presumably other Greek cities and provinces as well). No other Divine "ordinance" in Scripture is ever referred to as a "custom" or "habit" (sunetheia). Thus, I submit that Paul distinguishes the veiling of women (as a "custom" within Greek society at large) in 1 Corinthians 11:16 from the regulated Divine "ordinances" or "traditions" referred to in 1 Corinthians 11:2,23 (which the covered head of a woman or the uncovered head of a man in 1 Corinthians 11:3-16 is never said to be). I will have more to say about 1 Corinthians 11:16 when I come to your 8th argument.

I will stop there for now and allow you to reply to this my first response to your 1st argument from 1 Corinthians 11:2.

I look forward to our continued discussion of this matter in brotherly charity with the firm hope that such a discussion might lead to an organic union of churches and Christians within the Visible Church of Christ.

For the Cause of Christ,

Greg L. Price

_____

March 7, 2011

Dear ___,

I do appreciate the care that you and the elders are taking to study the matter of headcoverings. Whether we should be adding to or taking away from the duties that are ours in worship, it is very serious business (Deuteronomy 12:32).

If I might take a few minutes to comment on the three possibilities you mentioned with regard to the omission of headcoverings as a prescribed act of worship in the Westminster Standards. ___, I thought synthesizing the possible explanations for this omission from the Westminster Standards was very helpful. You stated in your email (dated 2/15/11):

> We all agreed that it was certainly a curiosity that headcovering was never mentioned by the church during the writing of the Standards. I put three questions to my elders, I asked them if they thought that the writers of the Westminster Standards, (1) overlooked the practice (which seems highly unlikely), (2) or it was so obvious it need hardly be mentioned (also pretty unlikely), or (3) it was roundly agreed that headcovering was cultural and therefore no arguments needed to take place.

If I might briefly respond to each of these three possible explanations for the omission of headcoverings within the Westminster Standards as a prescribed duty in worship, I will proceed to do so.

Option One

The first option, the writers of the Westminster Standards "overlooked the practice."

I would submit that this position is not tenable since the divines actually did NOT omit the mention of headcoverings in the Westminster Standards — they included the mention of headcoverings as a proof-text (1 Corinthians 11:13,14) within the *Confession of Faith* (1:6). And as an approved proof-text, the divines clearly did not place the use of headcoverings in worship as a regulated act in worship authorized in Scripture, but rather under "some circumstances concerning the worship of God . . . common to human actions and societies." In other words, there really is not a total silence on the part of the divines in regard to the use of headcoverings in worship. To the contrary, they not only mention headcoverings, but place them outside the acts of worship that are specifically to be regulated by Holy Scripture. Thus, I must conclude that the divines did NOT overlook the practice within the Westminster Standards.

Option Two

The second possibility you mention is that "it was so obvious it need hardly be mentioned". I
would submit this option is likewise not tenable unless one believes it is the only prescribed act in worship that was so obvious that it need not be mentioned. For was it not even more obvious from a study of Scripture (both Old and New Testaments) that the use of prayer in worship and the use of reading and explication of the Word of God in worship were prescribed parts of worship specifically ordained by God? And yet, as obvious as these two regulated parts of worship are in Scripture, they are nevertheless included among the various lists of acts/parts of worship mentioned in the Westminster Standards. In fact, what regulated part of worship would any of us say was so obvious to the divines that they decided not to include it within their lists of regulated worship (whether in the *Confession of Faith*, the *Directory For the Public Worship of God*, or the *Form of Presbyterial Church-Government*)? The lists of regulated acts of worship are very complete and thorough in the Westminster Standards.

Furthermore, how would we respond if someone presented the same argument for the omission of instruments in worship from the text of the Westminster Standards? Should we be persuaded by the same argument from silence that the omission of instruments as a prescribed part of New Covenant worship in the Westminster Standards was due to the fact that the use of instruments was so obvious that it need hardly be mentioned? Such an argument from silence would lead to a host of acts being incorporated into worship if one believed that a regulated act of worship was omitted by the Westminster divines simply because it was so obvious that it need hardly be mentioned (e.g. the use of incense in worship, the use of holy water, the use of an altar, and the use of choirs could all find warrant in our worship services by a similar argument from silence in the Westminster Standards). Rather than assume that a prescribed act of worship was intentionally omitted (or any number of prescribed acts of worship were intentionally omitted) by the Westminster divines, I conclude they did not intend to leave such important matters as the worship of God to guess-work in what they penned, but rather they listed for us in the Westminster Standards what they clearly believed alone had biblical warrant to be used in the public worship of God.

Option Three

The third possibility ("it was roundly agreed that head-covering was cultural and therefore no arguments needed to take place.") is that which fits with the evidence both within the Westminster Standards and within the ecclesiastical practice of the Westminster divines at that time in the use of headcoverings. The Westminster divines did not use the terms "cultural circumstances" or "customs" within the Standards, but did use language pointing to the same reason for Paul's direction in regard to the use of headcoverings in 1 Corinthians 11:13,14 (proof-text for *Confession of Faith*, 1:6): "some circumstances concerning the worship of God" which are "common to human actions and societies." These acts in worship included here in *Confession of Faith* (1:6) would include cultural acts that may change from society to society (when/if a headcovering should be used for men or women or both; what postures are appropriate for prayer, preaching, singing; what outward forms of greeting are appropriate, whether kissing, embracing, or hand-shaking on the part of both genders; what outward forms of grief/sorrow are appropriate, whether covering the head, rending a garment, crying loudly or quietly; what outward forms of loving service to one another are appropriate, whether washing the feet of the disciples or some other act, etc.). For the reasons stated in my previous letter (dated February 4, 2011), and for the insuperable problems with the other two options addressed in this letter, I submit we are cast upon this third option as the only viable consideration.

Thanks again, ___, for allowing me this opportunity.

For the Cause of Christ,

Greg L. Price

March 7, 2011

Dear ___,

Thank you so very much for your response and questions of clarification. This makes our discussion all the more beneficial not only for us, but also for anyone else who is following this discussion.

In the first place, perhaps it would be helpful to make certain distinctions between customary signs (and practices) and regulative principle signs (and practices).

1. On the one hand, customary signs (and practices) have a place in worship not because they have been specifically appointed by God for such a sacred use in worship, but because they have a civil use in society at large in maintaining some degree of order and uniform practice within a cultural setting. Thus, to alter or change that customary sign (or practice) would introduce confusion and disorder into the worship of God. For example, if it is a customary practice to have **gender-segregated** seating in civil public meetings (with the men sitting near the front and the women sitting near the back) as an expression of the respective place and order within society between men and women, then such a customary practice ought to be used in the public meetings of the church as well. For to introduce **gender-integrated** seating within worship in a cultural setting where **gender-segregated** seating is practiced in a society at large would bring great confusion and disorder into the worship of God. Or, if it was a customary sign and practice within society at large to bow as a sign of submission and respect when speaking to a superior, then it would introduce confusion into the worship of God to stand upright in prayer when addressing God, the Divine Superior. On the other hand, regulative principle signs (and practices) are used in worship specifically because they are set apart by the Lord for a holy use and appointed for a sacred use in the worship of God and not for a civil use in society at large. For example, the sacred signs and seals of Baptism and the Lord's Supper do not have a customary practice outside of worship in society at large, but only a regulated use in worship alone (so likewise prayer, preaching, singing psalms, etc).

2. On the one hand, customary signs (and practices) are alterable within churches from nation to nation; on the other hand regulative principle signs (and practices) are not alterable within churches from nation to nation.

3. On the one hand, customary signs (and practices) may express **general principles** that are taught by the Light of Nature within man (e.g. gender distinctions and roles, order, submission, charity, respect, etc.). On the other hand, regulative principle signs (and practices) express **specifically revealed truths** taught in Scripture (e.g. the cleansing of sin, union and communion with Christ etc.).

In the second place, yes, in answer to your question, I would understand all "customary signs" as falling under the confessional category of "circumstances common to human actions and societies". For a customary sign (or practice) first obtains a general usage among the actions of humans within society at large. As Calvin indicates in his Commentary on 1 Corinthians, a custom is that which is "confirmed by length of time and common use" within a society (cf. footnote on 1 Corinthians 11:15). This is the very definition and meaning of "custom".

In the third place, I distinguish between the Light of Nature revealed within the very constitution of man and between outward customary signs that teach those Light of Nature principles. On the one hand, the Light of Nature is that knowledge of the Law of Nature within man that reflects (to some degree) general moral principles. Those general moral principles revealed by the Light of Nature within man are unalterable from nation to nation, from culture to culture, from church to church. On the other hand, the customary sign is the outward sign or practice within a given society that may reflect that moral principle revealed by the Light of Nature within man. For example, **the inward light of nature** teaches gender distinctions, whereas **the outward customary practice** within the Corinthians society that expressed the respective roles of men and women was the covered head for women and the uncovered head for men in public. Likewise **the inward light of nature** teaches the moral principle of headship and submission within the home, whereas **the outward customary sign** (and practice) of a servant to bow to his master, or for a son to bow to his father within ancient cultures are clearly distinguishable the one from the other. Thus, I would not understand that moral principles taught by Light of Nature differ from one society to another (even though the degree of light that one society may have over another may differ) or from one church to another, even though the outward customary sign within one society (and therefore within a church in that society) may differ from another society (and therefore from another church in that society) in expressing the same moral principle taught by the Light of Nature.

In the fourth place, I will try to fill out for you very briefly the three following categories that you have outlined in your email. Your three listed categories in which you seek clarification are: Regulative Principle of Worship, Light of Nature, and Customary Signs.

1. "Regulative Principle of Worship – i.e. psalm singing, reading of the Word, Preaching of the Word, prayer, etc." This category looks good with the parts of worship that you have included after it.

2. "Light of Nature – i.e. time of meeting, type of seating, etc." This category seems to need some clarification (at least from my perspective). For as I understand it, the

items that you have listed after "Light of Nature" (time of meeting, type of seating) are NOT specifically the general moral principles themselves that are taught by the Light of Nature within man. To the contrary, the general moral principles that are taught by the Light of Nature within man are order, edification, and charity rather than "time of meeting, type of seating, etc." In other words, the time of meeting and the type of seating are matters within a society in general that are to be ordered by the Light of Nature (but are not the Light of Nature themselves), or are to be ordered by the general principles of the Word, or are to be ordered by those actions that are common to human societies. The Light of Nature teaches that public meetings should meet in an orderly and edifying manner for all in attendance. But the Light of Nature is not "the time of meeting" or the "type of seating." The "time of meeting" and the "type of seating" are rather the customary practices that are common to human actions and societies.

3. "Customary signs – i.e. (Gillespie) headcovering, _____, _____." It is the third category that you have listed, "Customary signs" and practices in society at large, that is used by churches within that society to determine what would be the most orderly, the most edifying, and the most charitable practices for the "time of meeting, type of seating, etc." As for a couple more examples of "customary signs and practices", I would suggest the examples I used above: gender-segregated seating in public places, and bowing to superiors (also the holy kiss and foot washing are also examples of customary signs and practices).

___, I hope this is helpful to some degree in clarifying these three categories you mentioned. Feel free to follow-up with further questions, if it is still not clear to you.

In the fifth place, ___, you state,

> I agree that the historical testimony of the
> Westminster Assembly, especially argu-
> ing from silence (and one proof text) leans
> towards a belief that the Westminster As-
> sembly treated headcovering as a cultural
> practice.

When you use the words "**leans toward** a belief that the
Westminster Assembly treated headcovering as a cultural practice" (bold added), it sounds a little tentative, as
if there might be another position that has some degree
of credibility. I would ask, Is there any other position
that the Westminster divines might have embraced that
you think has *any plausibility* in dealing with the complete omission of headcoverings in any section of the
Standards that addresses regulated worship (whether
The Westminster Confession of Faith, or *The Directory For the
Public Worship of God*, or *The Form of Presbyterial Church
Government*), or has *any plausibility* in dealing with the
placement of 1 Corinthians 11:13,14 under the category of
"circumstances common to human actions and societies"
(*Westminster Confession of Faith*, 1:6)?

In the sixth place, ___, you state in your last paragraph
the following:

> I will remain open minded about the use
> of the word 'custom' in v. 16. I know that
> you would like to treat that at a further
> time. I am not aware of anything done in a
> worship service that would be done accord-
> ing to custom. Maybe you can think of an
> example of some other 'customs' that have

changed during various church ages.

I would ask if you had any disagreement with the argument that I presented in favor of headcoverings being addressed by Paul as a "custom"? In other words, if the churches do not have a custom of women praying uncovered in worship, then we may deduce that they had a "custom" of women praying covered in worship. I do not see how one avoids this deductive argument and conclusion. Which if true means then that Paul calls the covered head of a woman in worship a "custom", which is quite different from a regulated act in worship (see the distinctions I made above between regulated worship and customary signs and practices). As I also indicated above, seating (whether in chairs or on the ground, whether gender-segregated or gender-integrated), and gestures (whether bowing or standing in prayer, whether standing or sitting while preaching, whether giving or not giving a holy kiss), all of these are cultural practices that pertain to worship, and yet are alterable from age to age within churches depending upon the practices within society at large.

I will stop at this point, and wait to hear from you as to whether the matters needing clarification were sufficiently clarified in this response of mine.

For the Cause of Christ,

Greg L. Price

March 9, 2011

Dear ___,

I had one more argument that I wanted to add to our discussion surrounding 1 Corinthians 11:2. Sometimes refinements in arguments or a mental flash do not immediately appear, but come gradually. Thanks for considering this argument as well.

Yours,

Greg L. Price

ONE REMAINING ARGUMENT FROM 1 CORINTHIANS 11:2

___, your first argument from 1 Corinthians 11:2 was submitted in the following words:

> Paul begins chapter 11 v. 2 by praising
> those who kept the ordinances, but what
> ordinances? I understand the ordinances he
> is about to speak of, which are the proper
> use of headcovering, the proper obser-
> vance or the Lord's Supper, and proper use
> of spiritual gifts [from your email dated
> 1/20/11 — GLP].

I would like to submit one more argument from 1 Corinthians 11:2 before moving on to
1 Corinthians 11:3 that in my judgment further demonstrates that Paul DID NOT INTEND to include among the "ordinances" (or literally, "traditions") which the Corinthians were keeping and for which they were

praised anything mentioned by Paul in 1 Corinthians 11:3-16.

Once again, we consider 1 Corinthians 11:2: "Now I praise you, brethren, that ye remember me in all things, and keep the ordinances [*paradosis*—GLP], as I delivered [*paradidomi*—GLP] them to you."

First, undoubtedly Paul teaches that the Lord's Supper was such an "ordinance" (i.e. apostolic tradition received from Christ and delivered by the apostles to the church) when he states in 1 Corinthians 11:23: "For I have received of the Lord that which also I DELIVERED [*paradidomi* is used by Paul here in 1 Corinthians 11:23 and is the verbal form of the noun that is used in 1 Corinthians 11:2, *paradosis*, i.e. "ordinances"—GLP] unto you . . . ." Thus, at least in this instance of the Lord's Supper, we can be sure that there is an "ordinance" (apostolic tradition) addressed in 1 Corinthians 11-14. However, is this an "ordinance" for which Paul can praise the Corinthians for keeping as stated in 1 Corinthians 11:2? To the contrary, Paul DOES NOT PRAISE the Corinthians, because they were NOT KEEPING this "ordinance" of the Lord's Supper: "Now in this that I declare unto you I PRAISE YOU NOT, that ye come together not for the better, but for the worse" (1 Corinthians 11:17).

Second, in 1 Corinthians 11:2, Paul states, "I praise you" (and that praise proceeds from the fact that the Corinthians remembered Paul and were keeping the "ordinances" that Paul delivered to them). However, in 1 Corinthians 11:17 Paul states, "I praise you NOT." Why? Because they were not keeping the "ordinance" (or apostolic tradition) of the Lord's Supper. The contrast could not be more clear in the Greek language. "I praise [*epaino*—GLP] you" in 1 Corinthians 11:2; and "I praise you NOT" [*ouk* *epaino* — GLP] in 1 Corinthians 11:17.

Third, in other words, here is just another reason why I submit that the "ordinances" (apostolic traditions) mentioned in 1 Corinthians 11:2 must be unnamed "ordinances" (apostolic traditions) that the Corinthians were actually keeping and for which they were sincerely praised by Paul.

Finally, whatever the "ordinances" the Corinthians were keeping and for which they were praised by Paul in 1 Corinthians 11:2, those "ordinances" could not be that for which the Corinthians are subsequently rebuked and corrected by Paul in 1 Corinthians 11:3-16, and are told that he does NOT praise them because they were not keeping them.

A Letter Responding to Argument #2 (1 Corinthians 11:3)

March 26, 2011

THE SECOND ARGUMENT FROM 1 CORINTHIANS 11:3

Dear ___,

Having completed our discussion of your 1st Argument (from 1 Corinthians 11:2), I now proceed to your 2nd Argument from 1 Corinthians 11:3, wherein you state the following:

> 2. The argument in v. 3 is rooted in nature, which does not change with culture. Christ is always the head of man, God the head of Christ and man the head of woman [from your email dated 1/20/11 – GLP].

Paul lays the foundation of headship and submission in 1 Corinthians 11:3, which forms the moral principle for what he will be addressing in regard to the "custom" (1 Corinthians 11:16) of women retaining the covered head when they leave the public secular arena and enter into the public sacred arena: "But I would have you know, that the head of every man is Christ; and the head of the woman is the man; and the head of Christ is God" (1 Corinthians 11:3).

41

First, note that 1 Corinthians 11:3 begins with the adversative "but" (*de*): "BUT I would have you know." This indicates that what Paul is about to say by way of correction is in contrast to the praise he just gave them for remembering him and keeping the UNSTATED "ordinances" that he had previously delivered to them (1 Corinthians 11:2). This is just another indication that Paul's rebuke and correction in regard to the headcovering (1 Corinthians 11:3-16) was not included among the "ordinances" which they were keeping and for which he praised them
(1 Corinthians 11:2).

Second, it is a metaphorical use of the word "head" that is in view here (in 1 Corinthians 11:3) when Paul states "the HEAD of every man is Christ; and the HEAD of the woman is the man; and the HEAD of Christ is God" (1 Corinthians 11:3, emphases in caps added). Just as the "head" is literally positioned above the other members of the physical body, so the "head" is figuratively superior in rank in the three relationships described in 1 Corinthians 11:3: Christ is the head of every man; the man is the head of the woman; and God is the head of Christ.

Jesus Christ (as Mediatorial King) has been granted by the Father a headship over "all things" (Ephesians 1:22), which certainly includes a headship over all men. Just as God is not the head of Christ as Christ is the Son of God (for the Father, the Son, and the Holy Spirit are "one God, the same in substance, equal in power and glory" as summarized by the Answer given to Question 6 in the Westminster Shorter Catechism), but as Christ is the Son of Man (i.e. as Christ is Mediator), so Christ (as the Son of Man and as Mediatorial King) is the head of "every man" (i.e. every man is under the lordship of Christ as He is Mediatorial King appointed by God, just as every nation is under the lordship of Christ as He is Mediatorial King, according to Revelation 1:5). I submit that the headship of Christ over "every man" in 1 Corinthians 11:3 is not a spiritual or an ecclesiastical headship, but rather a universal headship over "every man" (without exception). When we find the use of "every man" in 1 Corinthians 11:4 ("Every man praying or prophesying"), "every man" is qualified by those who are "praying or prophesying." However, here in 1 Corinthians 11:3, "every man" is unqualified, and therefore, I submit it refers to the Mediatorial Headship of Christ over "every man" without exception (whether Christian, Jew, or heathen). And likewise, I submit that the headship of man over woman refers to men and women (without qualification, whether Christian, Jew, or heathen). This point is very significant and needs to be understood, because it demonstrates that Paul is not immediately concerned (in 1 Corinthians 11:3) with relationships within the Church or within Church meetings, but is rather immediately concerned to formulate universal MORAL/THEOLOGICAL principles that relate to all men and women (whether they are Christians or not, whether they are in the Church or outside the Church). In other words, these universal moral principles of headship/submission among men and women relate to cultural society as well as to ecclesiastical society. Moreover, these examples of headship/submission (cited by Paul in 1 Corinthians 11:3) would also likely have encouraged the Corinthian women to understand that they were not the only ones who were under the headship of another. Yes, women are under the headship of men, but men are under the headship of Christ (as Mediatorial King), and Christ (as Mediatorial King) is under the headship of God. Thus, headship does not mean superiority in regard to essence, but rather superiority in regard to rank. Just as Christ is not inferior to God in regard to the Divine Nature, so women are not inferior to men in regard to their human nature—there is simply a Divine order which God has established in His moral universe from the time of creation as it relates to the headship of men and the submission of women.

Carefully note that from the very outset of Paul's argument in 1 Corinthians 11, the moral principles of headship/submission among men and women relate not simply to the Church, but to all society at large; and therefore, I propose at this point that if the moral principles of headship/submission among men and women relate to the whole Corinthian society (rather than simply to the Corinthian Church), the outward sign of that headship/submission (namely, the uncovered head for men/the covered head for women) also relates to the cultural context of the whole Corinthian society (rather than solely to the Corinthian Church). Which would mean that if one believes that a covered head is now required for a Christian woman in the public meetings of the church (due to the moral principle of submission) and an uncovered head is now required for a Christian man in the public meetings of the church (due to the moral principle of headship), then it would also mean that a covered head is now required for all women in public society (due to the universal, moral principle of submission) and an uncovered head is now required for all men in public society (due to the universal, moral principle of headship). For clearly, the moral principles of headship/submission are not based upon the Regulative Principle of Worship; otherwise they would not apply outside the assembly of the church or outside the realm of Christians. But clearly the moral principles of headship/submission do relate to the Divine order that God has established in secular society as well as in sacred society. Thus, to limit universal moral principles of headship/submission that relate to all men and women (and their corresponding outward signs of the uncovered head and covered head) to only ecclesiastical meetings is (in my opinion) unwarranted and unreasonable to suppose. I would submit that the only reason why Paul brings the matter of the uncovered head for men and the covered head for women to the attention of the Corinthian Church (in 1 Corinthians 11) was because the women were taking off their headcovering when they entered into the assembly of the church (likely this was an ancient feminist movement on the part of women who perhaps sought to erroneously portray the truth that there was neither male nor female in Christ, Galatians 3:28). It would seem to me that one can only establish that the uncovered head of men and the covered head of women relate only to ecclesiastical meetings, by first establishing that the universal moral principles of headship/submission are based upon the Regulative Principle of Worship which relates only to ecclesiastical society (which obviously cannot be done, because the headship of man and the submission of women go all the way back to creation, 1 Corinthians 11:7-9, and relate to all nations, cultures, and societies).

Third, the headship of the man over the woman goes back to creation (as was just stated above). But Paul is not teaching that the headcovering itself is a creation ordinance, but that the universal moral principles of headship in men and of submission in women are moral principles founded in the Law of Nature stretching back to creation (and taught by the Light of Nature within man to varying degrees, even if sin has greatly distorted the Light of Nature within man). For Eve was not created wearing a headcovering, and Eve did not wear a headcovering in worship there in the Garden of Eden (even though the universal moral principles of headship/submission were clearly established at the point of their creation, as we see in 1 Corinthians 11:7-9). For both Adam

45

and Eve were created naked, and were naked the entire time while in the Garden of Eden (Genesis 2:25). Thus, there is no dispute as far as I am concerned with your statement, ___: "The argument in v. 3 is rooted in nature, which does not change with culture. Christ is always the head of man, God the head of Christ and man the head of woman." What I do dispute is that this argument that Paul uses in 1 Corinthians 11:3 proves that the headcovering itself is "rooted in nature" (rather than rooted in custom). The universal moral principle of male headship and of female submission is indeed rooted in nature, but not the headcovering itself (otherwise Eve would have been created with a headcovering upon her head or commanded to place a headcovering upon her head when she worshipped there in the Garden of Eden). Thus, because Eve was not created with a headcovering or commanded to wear a headcovering when she worshipped, we may conclude that it is the universal moral principle of headship/submission (which relates to all cultures, all societies, and all churches) rather than the headcovering itself (which relates to only particular cultures, societies, and churches) that Paul specifically has in view in 1 Corinthians 11:3.

Fourth, it has already been argued in the first letter (dated February 4, 2011) from a contrast of 1 Corinthians 11:2 in the use of the word "ordinances" (i.e. apostolic traditions) with 1 Corinthians 11:16 in the use of the word "custom" (i.e. customary signs), that the headcovering fell under the category of a customary sign according to Paul, not under the category of an "ordinance" (whether a creation ordinance or a regulative principle ordinance). Thus, Paul is NOT teaching that the use of the uncovered head for men and the covered head for women is universal and unalterable, but that the moral principles of headship/submission are universal and unalterable. When we

46

confuse this most important distinction at the very outset of Paul's discussion, we will inevitably fail to distinguish an unalterable universal moral principle revealed within man by the Light of Nature from an alterable non-universal cultural sign outwardly practiced by society at large. Just as the unalterable moral principle of loving service to the brethren is to be distinguished from the alterable cultural practice of washing the feet of Christ's disciples (John 13:14,15), so the unalterable moral principles of headship/submission are to be distinguished from the alterable cultural signs of the uncovered head/covered head.

Fifth, let me elaborate on this point by using a different outward cultural sign. If within a cultural context, it is customary to have gender-segregated seating in public meetings, so that a clear distinction between men and women (and the headship of men and the submission of women) is outwardly demonstrated in public meetings, then that cultural practice should not be overturned when the Church of Jesus Christ gathers for public worship. Incidentally, **gender-segregated seating** was the ordinary practice in Christian churches from ancient days to at least the early 18th century, even as it was generally the case in civil, secular public meetings from ancient times. No doubt, in a culture where there is gender-segregated seating in public meetings (in both civil and ecclesiastical meetings), it would become a scandalous matter that would need to be addressed by the appropriate church court if a congregation decided to practice mixed seating (i.e. gender-integrated seating), thus removing such cultural practices intended to distinguish between men and women (and intended to portray the headship of men and the submission of women) — not because gender-segregated seating itself is a creation ordinance or a regulative principle ordinance, but because the moral principles of maintaining male-female distinctions and maintaining the headship of men and the submission of women is taught by the Light of Nature and displayed in that cultural practice of gender-segregated seating. The same is true in regard to the customary practice (1 Corinthians 11:16) of headcoverings. The reason it was a matter that Paul needed to address in 1 Corinthians 11 is not because the headcovering itself was a creation ordinance or a regulative principle ordinance, but because in that cultural setting in Corinth, for a woman to remove the customary sign of her submission to man when she entered into the public church meetings was to undermine the moral principle of male headship and female submission which was taught by the Light of Nature and portrayed by the customary sign of the headcovering within the Corinthian society at large.

Thus, ___, we must be clear at the outset that we are properly distinguishing the alterable customary sign from the unalterable moral principle, or we will end up with the wrong conclusions as to what Paul is saying. Even of greater significance (as shepherds of Christ's sheep), we would be imposing an alterable customary sign (as if it were an unalterable sacred sign) upon the consciences of the sheep when there is no warrant for doing so (no matter how well-intentioned we may be).

___, I will stop there in responding to your 2nd Argument from 1 Corinthians 11. I look forward to your response as you have the time.

Yours for the Cause of Christ,

Greg L. Price

A Letter Responding to Argument #3 (1 Corinthians 11:5)

April 17, 2011

THE THIRD ARGUMENT FROM 1 CORINTHIANS 11:5

Dear ___,

I move now to your 3rd Argument which is taken from 1 Corinthians 11:5 wherein you state:

> 3. Paul says that a women [sic.] is shamed (v. 5) by failing to wear a headcovering, as if she were shaven. Paul seems to indicate she would naturally be shamed in any culture [from your email dated 1/20/11 — GLP].

First, Paul moves now from having just set forth a universal MORAL/THEOLOGICAL principle of headship that addresses "every man" (in every culture without qualification, whether he be Christian, Jew, or heathen) in 1 Corinthians 11:3 ("the head of EVERY MAN is Christ") to applying that universal MORAL/THEOLOGICAL principle of headship to a specific case within the public assemblies of the Church of Corinth ("EVERY MAN PRAYING OR PROPHESYING, having his head covered, dishonoreth his head" 1 Corinthians 11:4). For surely, if the universal MORAL/THEOLOGICAL principle of headship applies to "every man" (in every culture without qualification, whether he be Christian, Jew, or heathen) in 1 Corinthians 11:3 ("the head of EVERY MAN is Christ"), then certainly that universal MORAL/THEOLOGICAL principle must necessarily apply to Christian men meeting in the public assemblies of the Church of Corinth ("EVERY MAN PRAYING OR PROPHESYING" 1 Corinthians 11:4). Specifically, every Christian man who gathers for worship in the Church of Corinth with a veil hanging down from his head (thus mimicking the cultural dress of Corinthian women in that society) dishonors his Head, Christ (1 Corinthians 11:3), and brings gender confusion into the House of God. For a man to cover his head with a veil in the Corinthian society was in effect to take upon himself the customary sign of female submission, and for a man to bring that customary sign of female submission into the Church of Christ was to further aggravate his sin by dishonoring Christ, and by disrupting and confusing the Divine order in the very worship of God (who established that order of male headship and female submission from the very creation of man and woman).

Whether some men in the Corinthian Church were actually wearing a veil in worship is not clear (though it is possible that such was the case since Paul addresses the men first and the women second), or whether Paul proposes this scenario as a hypothetical case with regard to men before directly addressing the actual case of abuse by women, in either case, the respective apostolic applications to men and women in the Corinthian Church is clear — Christian men ought not to take upon themselves the customary sign of female submission (the veiled head within the Corinthian society), nor ought Christian women to take upon themselves the customary sign of male headship (the unveiled head within the Corinthian society).

Whether "every man praying or prophesying" refers only to the ministers who alone prayed and prophesied publicly, or whether "every man praying or prophesying" refers to all the men in the congregation who prayed and prophesied representatively through the minister, the point of Paul remains the same: men ought not to take upon themselves the customary sign of female submission (the veiled head within the Corinthian society). Clearly, the Scripture does teach that the minister serves in a representative capacity when he leads in worship as the voice of many (rather than merely as the voice of one): "For every high priest taken from among men is ordained FOR MEN [i.e. "on behalf of men" as men's representative before God — GLP] in things pertaining to God" Hebrews 5:1. Likewise, Paul infers later on in 1 Corinthians 14 that the whole congregation was represented in the praying and prophesying of the minister (as the voice of many), for it was necessary for the minister who spoke in tongues publicly (by way of a miraculous gift from the Holy Spirit) to also interpret what he spoke in a foreign language so that all (even the unlearned) could say "Amen" at the conclusion of the giving of thanks to the Lord in the foreign language ("Else when thou shalt bless with the spirit, how shall he that occupieth the room of the unlearned say Amen at thy giving of thanks, seeing he understandeth not what thou sayest?" 1 Corinthians 14:16). Thus, the whole congregation could be said to be praying or prophesying when the minister was praying or prophesying; and thus, Paul's instruction in regard to men (in 1 Corinthians 11:4) may not only apply to the minister who is praying and prophesying publicly, but also to all the men in the congregation who representatively pray and prophesy through the minister.

Paul states that the man who prays and prophesies in the public worship of God with his head covered "dishonoreth his head" (1 Corinthians 11:4). Paul now ties together the specific ecclesiastical case of headship found in 1 Corinthians 11:4 to the general MORAL/THEOLOGICAL principle of headship found in 1 Corinthians 11:3; for the "head" that was dishonored or shamed by a Christian man who appeared in the Corinthian Church wearing the customary sign of female submission within the Corinthian society (i.e. the headcovering) was his Head, Christ (rather than his own literal head). It is a far more egregious aggravation of sin to dishonor and shame Christ, the Mediatorial King of all creation, than it is to simply dishonor and shame one's own head. The fact that 1 Corinthians 11:3 has specifically used the term "head" three times in a figurative sense should guide our interpretation of the word "head" in 1 Corinthians 11:4, when Paul states that a man who appears in the public meetings of the church wearing the customary sign of female submission "dishonoreth his head." Why make such a significant MORAL/THEOLOGICAL point in 1 Corinthians 11:3 about headship (and in particular, "the head of every man is Christ"), and then entirely disregard this very MORAL/THEOLOGICAL principle in the very next verse (1 Corinthians 11:4)? It may very well be true that a Christian man appearing in the public worship of God wearing the customary sign (within the Corinthian society) of female submission (i.e. the covered head) would bring dishonor and shame upon his own head (i.e. upon himself), but that is not the primary point that Paul is seeking to make here in 1 Corinthians 11:4. However, the point Paul seeks to make is that dishonor and shame are brought upon the name of Christ who is the "head of every man" (1 Corinthians 11:3) by such actions on the part of Christian men in the public worship of God. Why would Christ be put to shame by a Christian man who appeared in the public worship of God in Corinth wearing the customary sign (within the Corinthian society) of female submission? Because when a man (who is under the headship of Christ according to 1 Corinthians 11:3) appeared in the public worship of God with the customary sign of female submission, he mocked and disgraced Christ, his Head, who as Mediatorial King was given lordship over men that men might likewise reflect the image and glory of God in their loving headship over women (1 Corinthians 11:7). When the inferior does what is shameful in public, does it not likewise bring the greatest shame upon the superior? When children act shamefully and disrespectfully in public, does it not bring the greatest public shame upon the parents? In fact, the whole Divine order of headship revealed in 1 Corinthians 11:3 might as well be overthrown. For if one link of the Divine order of headship may be broken (the man's headship over the woman), why not the other links as well (Christ's headship over every man, and God's headship over Christ)? Thus, I submit, it is the shame brought upon Christ (as a far more aggravated offense than merely the shame brought upon his own literal head) that is distinctly in view in 1 Corinthians 11:4.

Second, Paul then moves from addressing Christian men to addressing Christian women as they appear in the public worship of God in 1 Corinthians 11:5,6: "But every woman that prayeth or prophesieth with her head uncovered dishonoreth her head: for that is even all one as if she were shaven. For if the woman be not covered, let her also be shorn: but if it be a shame for a woman to be shorn or shaven, let her be covered." ___, it is from these verses that you have specifically drawn your 3rd Argument. Allow me to ask a couple questions (and provide answers) based on what you have stated in your 3rd Argument.

Question #1: Who does Paul infer is shamed by the Christian woman who removes her headcovering when she assembles for the public worship of God in Corinth — the woman herself or men? In other words, who is the "head" that Paul has in view when he states in 1 Corinthians 11:5, "But every woman that prayeth or prophesieth with her head uncovered dishonoreth her head"? The woman's own literal head? Or men as the Divinely ordained head of women?

From your 3rd Argument, ___, you have taken the view that Paul infers in 1 Corinthians 11:5 that shame falls merely upon the Christian woman's OWN HEAD (i.e. upon herself) if she removes her headcovering upon entering the assembly of the Corinthian Church for public worship (and thus appears in the public worship of God in the customary sign of male headship, i.e. the uncovered head): "Paul says that a women [sic.] is shamed (v. 5) by failing to wear a headcovering, as if she were shaven" [from your email dated 1/20/11 — GLP]. I would submit that just as "his head" in 1 Corinthians 11:4 has primary reference to Christ, who is man's figurative Head, according to the MORAL/THEOLOGICAL principle found in 1 Corinthians 11:3 ("the head of every man is Christ"), so likewise "her head" in 1 Corinthians 11:5 has primary reference to man (in a general sense, and to the fathers and husbands in a particular sense), who is woman's figurative head, according to the MORAL/THEOLOGICAL principle found in 1 Corinthians 11:3 ("the head of the woman is the man"). Once again, this is not to deny that when Christian women gathered for the public worship of God in Corinth appearing in the customary sign of male headship (i.e. the uncovered head) that they brought shame upon their own heads for portraying themselves as men. But I would submit that the shame brought upon their own heads was not the most significant shame involved, nor the point that Paul was making in 1 Corinthians 11:5. On the contrary, the most aggravated shame was directed toward men (in a general sense, and to fathers and husbands in a particular sense). For the Divine order of headship related in 1 Corinthians 11:3 ("the head of the woman is the man") should likewise govern who the woman's head is in 1 Corinthians 11:5 ("But every woman that prayeth or prophesieth with her head uncovered dishonoreth her head"), just as 1 Corinthians 11:3 ("the head of every man is Christ") governs who is man's Head in 1 Corinthians 11:4 ("Every man praying or prophesying, having his head covered, dishonoreth his head"). It is one thing for an inferior to bring shame upon oneself by one's own actions, but it is another thing (and a greatly aggravated offense) to bring shame upon one's lawful superior appointed by God from the creation of the world.

As Calvin has observed from this text: "Now then, when a woman acts this way, she dishonors every man on earth" (*Men, Women and Order in the Church, Three Sermons by John Calvin*, Presbyterian Heritage Publications, p. 26).To bring shame upon the man by her appearing in public worship in the customary sign of male headship (i.e. the uncovered head) was also to strike at God who ordained male headship from the very beginning (as Paul will next make clear in 1 Corinthians 11:7-10). Once again, remember that Paul introduces in 1 Corinthians 11:3 the matter of headship with three separate cases where this MORAL/THEOLOGICAL truth applies (the headship of Christ over every man, the headship of the man over the woman, and the headship of God over Christ). But if Paul never applies this general MORAL/THEOLOGICAL truth to a specific case (as in 1

Corinthians 11:4-6), then one wonders for what purpose were these MORAL/THEOLOGICAL truths concerning headship/submission introduced at the very beginning of this section. Surely, the Holy Spirit did not intend to introduce general MORAL/THEOLOGICAL principles (in 1 Corinthians 11:3) without specific application to the particular ecclesiastical cases at issue (in 1 Corinthians 11:4-6).

Under this first question, perhaps it would also be appropriate at this time to indicate that whether or not the Christian men in the Corinthian Church were guilty of wearing the customary sign of female submission (i.e. the covered head), it ought not to be doubted that Christian women in the Corinthian Church were actually guilty (and so was the Corinthian church court for tolerating it) of appearing in the public worship of God in the customary sign of male headship (i.e. the uncovered head). For after 1 Corinthians 11:4, nothing more is specifically stated by Paul about the shame of the covered head of Christian men in the public assembly of the Church of Corinth, but the remainder of this section in 1 Corinthians 11:5-16 is directed toward the uncovered head of Christian women in the public assembly of the Church of Corinth.

Likewise under this first question, it is important to note that whether the Christian women in the Church of Corinth were specifically assuming the role of the minister in praying or prophesying publicly with an uncovered head, or whether the Christian women in the Church of Corinth were praying or prophesying representatively through the minister as the voice of many with an uncovered head, it is an egregious violation of Divine order for the woman (let alone a Christian woman) to appear in the Corinthian society at large in the customary sign of male headship (i.e. the uncovered head), but especially for the Christian woman to appear in the public worship of God in the customary sign of male headship (i.e. the uncovered head). If indeed Christian women were actually assuming the role of the minister by praying and prophesying publicly (as a voice of one), and were doing so using the customary sign of male headship (i.e. the uncovered head), the women who did so (and the ministers and elders that tolerated it) were guilty of even a more aggravated sin, which Paul later forbids in 1 Corinthians 14:34, "Let your women keep silence in the churches: for it is not permitted unto them to speak; but they are commanded to be under obedience, as also saith the law." This is to take the perversion of God's creation ordinance of male headship and female submission and to tempt God Himself by flaunting the inversion of woman's submission with man's headship in the very face of God within His public worship.

Question #2: When Paul states in 1 Corinthians 11:5 that every Christian woman in the Corinthian Church who prays or prophesies in the public worship of God with an uncovered head dishonors the man (i.e. her head), and that to do so is one and the same with the woman who either shaves or shears her head in order to look like a man (1 Corinthians 11:5,6), does Paul state or imply that this woman in the Church of Corinth who appears with an uncovered head in public worship "would naturally be shamed in any culture" (per the 3ʳᵈ Argument stated above)? What this question implies (due to the universality stated in the question, "in any culture"), is that the uncovered head of a woman (in and of itself) in public worship is either a violation of the **Regulative Principle of Worship** binding all Churches throughout the whole world in all ages, or a violation of the **Moral Law of God** binding all societies of men and women in all generations throughout history. These would seem to be the only two viable alternatives available, if one seeks to impute a universal shame to all women in all cultures and at all times who appear in the public worship of God with an uncovered head. For only the **Regulative Principle of Worship** and **God's Moral Law** can universally transcend all cultures and all times to bind the consciences of human beings.

___, I submit that Paul neither states nor implies that the uncovered head of a woman (in and of itself) within the public worship of God was a violation of the **Regulative Principle of Worship**, nor that it was (in and of itself) a violation of the **Moral Law of God**. Thus, if there is neither a violation of the **Regulative Principle of Worship** nor a violation of the **Moral Law of God** in the uncovered head of a woman (in and of itself) in public worship, there can be no UNIVERSAL shame caused by all Christian women (in every culture and at all times) who appear in the public worship of God with an uncovered head. There may be a local shame caused by Christian women (in certain cultural contexts) who appear in the public worship of God with an uncovered head, but not a universal shame.

Let's begin by considering the reasons why the uncovered head of a woman in the public worship of God is not a violation of the **Regulative Principle of Worship**, and therefore not a cause for universal shame.

1st, we would want to know when God instituted this alleged regulated practice of worship (the covered head of a woman) in His Word? Eve did not wear a headcovering when she worshipped God there in the Garden of Eden, for while they were in the Garden both Adam and Eve were naked (Genesis 2:25). In fact, there is nothing stated in the Old Testament about women being required by scriptural regulation to be covered in worship (or for that matter for men to be uncovered in worship). Since Paul states in 1 Corinthians 11:4-6 that men are to be uncovered at the precise same time that women are to be covered, if the uncovered head is not scripturally regulated in regard to all men in public worship in the Old Testament, then the covered head is likewise not scripturally regulated in regard to all women in public worship in the Old Testament. But clearly, men (at least the priests) were required by God in Scripture to cover their heads in worship (Exodus 28:4,37,40). Did the covered head for men in Old Testament worship bring universal shame and dishonor upon Christ, the head of all men in all cultures and in all generations? Obviously not, since God commanded men to be covered in public worship (at least the priests). Then the uncovered head of women in worship could not bring universal shame and dishonor upon men (who are the head of women) in all cultures and in all generations. In other words, if the uncovered head for men was not regulated in Old Testament worship, how could the necessary counterpart (i.e. the covered head for women) be regulated in Old Testament worship? If Paul was simply continuing a regulated part of worship (in the uncovered head of men and the covered head of women) from the Old Testament to the New Testament, why do Paul's statements contradict the Divine regulation found in the Old Testament?

2nd, there is complete silence in the New Testament with regard to the headcovering being a regulated practice in worship (unless of course that is Paul's point in 1 Corinthians 11). Jesus did not address the issue at all in requiring a headcovering for women in the public worship of God, nor did the other apostles do so in any of their epistles. If the veiling of women in worship and the non-veiling of men in worship is specifically regulated by

Scripture, it seems odd (to say the least) that this alleged regulated ordinance in worship was first introduced by Paul. Is there any other regulated practice in worship that is not found (as to essence) in Old Testament worship? All regulated parts and practices of New Covenant worship clearly had their origin in the Old Testament and were continued into the New Testament (such as prayer, the reading of Scripture, exposition of Scripture, psalm-singing, the benediction, the sacraments, oaths, vows, covenants, and even the Sabbath). And although the outward administration of the sacraments and the Sabbath has changed, they are in essence the same as that which was instituted in the Old Testament. However, if one changes the use of the covered head so that men (at least the priests, if not all men) are required to be covered in worship in the Old Testament, but required to be uncovered in the New Testament, one has altered the very essence of the meaning of the headcovering as taught by Paul (which is that the covered head is a sign of female submission, and the uncovered head is a sign of male headship). Is the veiling of women and the non-veiling of men in worship the only regulated act or practice in New Covenant worship that does not have its origin in the Old Testament? If there is one, what would it be? I do not believe the Scripture warrants such a position.

3rd, if one might seek to argue that Paul was the first one to institute (as a regulated practice in worship) the uncovered head for men and the covered head for women, how then was the Church of the Old Testament not commanded to do that in worship which is ALLEGED by many to be a creation ordinance (appealing to 1 Corinthians 11:7-9)? If Paul's exhortation (in 1 Corinthians 11) is a part of regulated worship, it should have bound not only the New Testament saints, but Old Testament saints as well. But it is demonstrable that such was not the case. Since there is no other command found in Scripture which requires men to be universally uncovered in worship and for women to be universally covered in worship, and since there are places in Scripture where men did not keep Paul's alleged command in worship (and did not do so with God's approval), how can we interpret Paul's command in 1 Corinthians 11 to be applied universally in all ecclesiastical circumstances? For the above three reasons, I submit that there cannot be UNIVERSAL shame (in all cultural contexts) due to every woman who does not wear a headcovering in the public worship of God, for the wearing of the headcovering in worship is not warranted by the **Regulative Principle of Worship** (which is clearly UNIVERSAL in its scope and application in regard to worship). And until the uncovered head for men and the covered head for women are clearly proven from Scripture to be governed by the **Regulative Principle of Worship**, we have no scriptural warrant to apply UNIVERSAL shame in all cultural contexts when women in worship pray and prophesy with an uncovered head.

Having considered the reasons why the uncovered head of a woman in the public worship of God is not a violation of the **Regulative Principle of Worship**, let's now consider the reasons why the uncovered head of a woman (in and of itself) in the public worship of God is not a violation of the **Moral Law of God**. For if there is UNIVERSAL shame upon a woman who prays and prophesies with an uncovered head, and if that UNIVERSAL shame is not due to a violation of the **Regulative Principles of Worship** (which is universal in its scope to all Christians in all cultural contexts when they gather for worship) as noted above, then the alleged UNIVERSAL shame of a woman who prays and prophesies with an uncovered head must be due to the **Moral Law of God** (which is universal in its scope to all men, women, and children in all cultural contexts in all generations, and the only other possible reason why there would be UNIVERSAL shame for the uncovered woman in worship). It should be observed that IF (for the sake of argument) God required by His **Moral Law** for all women (Christian and non-Christian alike) to cover their heads, such a requirement would not be limited to the public worship of God alone. But rather it would apply to all women (without exception) in all cultural contexts whenever they appear in public (or at least in all public meetings). And if this were the case, Christian women who removed their headcovering when entering into the public assembly of the saints would be in violation of **God's Moral Law** (which would in such a case bind all women whether in civil society or in ecclesiastical society).

The **1st** reason why the covered head of women (in and of itself) in all public contexts is not required by the **Moral Law of God** is that the covered head for women was certainly not a creation ordinance that bound Eve as a woman (even though the moral principle of submission to Adam did bind her and even though the **Moral Law of God** clearly bound her). For Adam and Eve were created naked (Genesis 2:25), and lived and worshipped in their nakedness without any garment upon their body (which includes the head) there in the Garden of Eden (even though the moral principle of male headship and female submission are inferred from the Genesis account: First, by the order of creation — first man, then woman; and second, by the origin of woman — she was taken from man, see 1 Corinthians 11:7-10). All of **God's Moral Law** bound Adam and Eve there in the Garden of Eden, and yet Eve did not cover her head. Thus, I submit that the covered head for women or the uncovered head for men is not comprehended under the **Moral Law of God**.

Neither is there any indication that God required Eve to cover her head when appearing in public after the fall (or for Adam to always appear in public with an uncovered head) after the fall. For carefully note that God made a "coat of skins" for both Adam and Eve after the fall (Genesis 3:21). He did not make a headcovering for Eve. IF (for the sake of argument) it was a universal moral requirement for women to be covered at all times in public and in all cultural contexts, God would have surely made a distinct article of clothing (i.e. the headcovering) for Eve as the representative for all women throughout the whole world. The Hebrew word for "coat" (in Genesis 3:21) means a "tunic" which was the ordinary garment for both men and women worn about the body. If the "coat" here refers to or includes a veil for a woman, it is the only place in Scripture where that Hebrew word for "coat" would bear that meaning. Furthermore, what God made for Eve (a coat), He also made for Adam (a coat). Thus, if God clothed Eve with a coat (and if that means God also made her a headcovering), then He also clothed Adam with a coat (and that also means God made him a headcovering as well). For what God made for the one, He made for the other (namely, a "coat"). One cannot distinguish here a difference in the clothing which God prepared for Eve as opposed to the clothing which God prepared for Adam. Thus, the Scripture knows nothing of **God's Moral Law** requiring all men to be uncovered when in public (both civilly and ecclesiastically) and requiring all women to be covered when in public (both civilly and ecclesiastically) at the creation of man and woman or at the fall of man and woman. Thus, the head-covering (in and of itself) does not fall under authority and regulation of **God's Moral Law**.

2nd, moving from the time of creation and the fall, we consider next the rest of the period of the Old Testament to see if warrant may be found from **God's Moral Law** for all men to be uncovered in public (both civilly and ecclesiastically) and all women to be covered in public (both civilly and ecclesiastically). REBEKAH was uncovered in the presence of the men who traveled with her until she saw Isaac, her future husband, at which time she covered herself with a veil (Genesis 24:65). How does this practice of Rebekah comport with what Paul says? Are women only to veil themselves when they are in the presence of their husbands (or future husbands)? If Rebekah's action here in veiling herself in the presence of her future husband is based upon the **Moral Law of God**, we might then conclude that when a woman's husband is not present, she is not required to veil herself, even if she is in a public meeting (whether civil or ecclesiastical). And if that is the case, then Paul is only addressing women in the congregation whose husbands were present in worship (but is neither addressing the women who were single nor the women whose husbands were not present in the public worship of God). But clearly Paul makes no such distinction with regard to women in the Corinthian Church, but is quite inclusive of all women in the Corinthian Church (whether married or single, whether her husband was present or not present in worship): "But EVERY WOMAN that prayeth and prophesieth with her head uncovered dishonoreth her head" (1 Corinthians 11:5). Thus, the example of Rebekah in covering herself in the presence of her future husband may certainly have conveyed in that cultural context a respect for and submission to her future husband, but it cannot be maintained with any consistency that Paul was teaching that women are only required to wear a headcovering (according to the **Moral Law of God**) when their husbands or future husbands were present. Again the fact that RUTH had a veil (Ruth 3:15) and that the beloved one of the king had a veil (Song of Solomon 5:7) does not prove that such was required by **God's Moral Law** — it may just as well indicate a cultural practice at that time. For if it was required by **God's Moral Law** for a woman to be covered whenever in public (both civilly and ecclesiastically), then it was likewise required by **God's Moral Law** for men to be uncovered whenever in public (both civilly and ecclesiastically) according to Paul's teaching which clearly states that at the precise same time that women are to be covered (1 Corinthians 11:5), men are likewise to be uncovered (1 Corinthians 11:4), due to the moral principles of headship and submission (stated in 1 Corinthians 11:3). But do we find men covered in the Old Testament in both civil and ecclesiastical settings? Yes, we do. For example, DAVID covered himself as he fled from Absalom (2 Samuel 15:30). In so doing, was David taking upon himself the sign of female submission and violating the **Moral Law of God**? SHADRACH, MESHACH, AND ABEDNEGO wore turbans in their civil life (Daniel 3:21). In so doing, were Shadrach, Meshach, and Abednego taking upon themselves the sign of female submission and violating the **Moral Law of God**? THE BRIDEGROOM wore a head-dress of some kind at his wedding (Isaiah 61:10). For the phrase "as a bridegroom decketh himself with ornaments" literally means "as a bridegroom adorns himself with a head-dress like a priest." The same word (translated "ornament" in Isaiah 61:10) is translated as "turban" in Ezekiel 24:17,23. In so doing, was the bridegroom taking upon himself the sign of female submission and violating the **Moral Law of God**? And the PRIESTS OF GOD covered themselves with mitres or bonnets as they worshipped the Lord (Exodus 28:4,40) as we have already noted above. These few examples illustrate that Paul's words to men (to be uncovered) and to women (to be covered) in the Church of Corinth could not be based upon the **Moral Law of God**, otherwise there is a contradiction in **God's Moral Law** as applied to the Old Testament and as applied to the New Testament (which we know is impossible, for it is impossible for God to lie or to deny Himself, 2 Timothy 2:13; Titus 1:2). Thus, since the words of Paul in requiring men to be uncovered in public worship at the exact same time that women are required to be covered in public worship neither fall under the **Regulative Principle of Worship** (which is UNIVERSAL in the public worship of all Christian churches in all ages) nor fall under the **Moral Law of God** (which is UNIVERSAL in all civil and ecclesiastical contexts for all people in all ages), we may conclude that there was no UNIVERSAL shame that resulted in all cultural contexts for women to pray and prophesy with their heads uncovered. It was not a UNIVERSAL shame that Paul addresses here in 1 Corinthians 11:5, but rather a LOCAL shame that resulted from women in the Church of Corinth appearing in public worship with the customary and cultural sign of male headship (i.e. the uncovered head).

Third (and finally), Paul moves FROM declaring that a woman who appears in the Corinthian assembly with the customary sign of male headship (the uncovered head) shames her head (i.e. all men in general and her father and/or husband specifically) in 1 Corinthians 11:5a TO now providing support (in 1 Corinthians 11:5b-6) for what he has just declared. The conjunction "for" begins the introduction of Paul's supporting statement: "FOR that is even all one as if she were shaven. FOR if the woman be not covered, let her also be shorn: but if be a shame for a woman to be shorn or shaven, let her be covered" (1 Corinthians 11:5b-6). Paul states that when a woman removes her headcovering upon entering the Corinthian assembly (thus appearing with the customary sign of male headship), she might as well have her head shaven (with a razor) or shorn (in a closely cut style), which were the distinctive hair styles of a man in the Corinthian society. The shaven or shorn styles for men were not unique to the Christian men in Corinth when they appeared in worship, but were the cultural style of men in the Corinthian society in general. Thus, Paul is really declaring that Christian women who want to appear in the assembly of the Corinthian Church looking like a man (which was true of the uncovered head in the Corinthian society) ought in all consistency to go all the way in shaming and disgracing all men (and their fathers and/or husbands in particular) not only within the Corinthian assembly specifically, but also to cut their hair to look like a man's shaven or shorn head in shaming and disgracing all men in general (and their fathers and/or husbands in particular). Paul is simply showing the Christian women in Corinth where their uncovered head in public worship logically and consistently leads them: to a shaven or shorn head that is not limited to public worship, but is seen by everyone in public society in general. Paul says in effect, "If you do not want to bring shame upon all men (including your fathers and husbands) by shaving or shearing your head to look like a man in public at all times, then stop uncovering your head in public worship and appearing in the customary sign of male headship. Continue to cover your head when you come into public worship as it was covered before you entered worship" (this is the emphasis of the present imperative, "let her continue to be covered" in   1 Corinthians 11:5, i.e. don't remove the headcovering once you have entered into the Church of Corinth, but continue to wear it when worshipping God).

Moreover, I submit that there is inferred in this supporting argument of Paul (in 1 Corinthians 11:5b-6) an analogy between the uncovered head of a man and the shaven or shorn head of a man that should not escape our notice.

Just as a shaven or shorn head of a man in Corinth did not apply only to public worship, but was the customary style for men in Corinthian society in general (in other words, a Corinthian man who was shaven or shorn was not only shaven or shorn after he entered into public worship, but would also have that same shaven or shorn head both BEFORE coming into public worship, DURING public worship, and AFTER leaving public worship), so also the uncovered head of a man should be parallel to that; for the uncovered head of a man in Corinth did not apply only to public worship, but was the customary sign for men in Corinthian society in general (in other words, a Corinthian man who was uncovered was not only uncovered when he entered into public worship, but would also have the same uncovered head both BEFORE coming into public worship, DURING public worship, and AFTER leaving public worship). Now let us fill out the analogy by applying what was just said about the man to the woman. Just as the long hair of a woman in Corinth did not apply only to public worship, but was the customary style of women in Corinthian society in general (in other words, a Corinthian woman with long hair not only had her long hair after she entered into public worship, but would also have that same long hair both BEFORE coming into public worship, DURING public worship, and AFTER leaving public worship), so also the covered head of a woman should be parallel to that; for the covered head of a woman in Corinth did not apply only to public worship, but was the customary sign for women in Corinthian society in general (in other words, a Corinthian woman who was covered was not only covered when she entered into public worship, but would also have the same covered head both BEFORE coming into public worship, DURING public worship, and AFTER leaving public worship). Paul's analogy here in Corinthian society between the uncovered head of a man and the shaved or shorn head of a man, and between the covered head of a woman and the long hair of a woman further substantiates the fact that the uncovered head of men and the covered head of women were not limited to the public worship of God (i.e. the **Regulative Principle of Worship**) any more than the shaved/shorn head of a man and the long hair of a woman were limited to the public worship of God (i.e. the **Regulative Principle of Worship**). These were all applicable to the Corinthian society in general, but the reason why Paul addresses the issue in 1 Corinthians 11 is because it was specifically in the ecclesiastical arena (and not in civil arena) that the uncovering of the Christian women in Corinth was occurring. It was in the public worship of God that the women were laying aside their distinctive customary sign for the customary sign of the man. This brought confusion, schism, and disruption into the very place (the public worship of God) where peace, purity, and unity should reign.

___, before ending this response to your 3rd Argument, I think it is worth observing that the covered head of a woman was a fabric covering distinct and separate from her hair, rather than a reference to her hair (i.e. her long hair that was bound up upon her head). I know you understand this to be the case as well, though there are scholars who specifically identify the covered head of a woman as the long hair of a woman (in other words, the covered head of a woman is the very same thing as the long hair of a woman). First, I submit Paul makes this distinction between the fabric covering of a woman and the long hair of a woman abundantly clear in 1 Corinthians 11:5b, when he declares: "for that is even all one as if she were shaven." In other words, the shameful, uncovered head of a woman in 1 Corinthians 11:5a is "all one as if she were shaven" (1 Corinthians 11:5b).

This only makes sense if Paul is comparing a woman who has removed her headcovering to a woman who has shaved her head. If the uncovered head of a woman does not refer to removing a veil, but rather means a shaven head, then this nonsensical statement would follow: "The shameful shaven head of a woman (1 Corinthians 11:5a) is "all one as if she were shaven" (1 Corinthians 11:5b). The same absurd reasoning would likewise be unjustly imputed to the inspired pen of Paul in 1 Corinthians 11:6 where if the uncovered head means once again a shaved or shorn head, Paul would be declaring, "For if the woman be not covered (i.e. if the woman be shaved or shorn), let her also be shorn" (in other words, "If a woman have her hair shorn, let her have her hair shorn"). Only when one understands that Paul is comparing (not identifying) an uncovered head with a shaved or shorn head can any sense be made out of what Paul is declaring. Thus, Paul addresses the Corinthians women in 1 Corinthians 11:5-6 who were removing a fabric headcovering when they entered into the public worship of God, and commands them, to continue to wear the same fabric headcovering in public worship that they had been wearing before entering into the Christian assembly in Corinth.

___, thank you once again, my brother, for allowing me the opportunity to submit to you my response to the 3rd Argument you submitted to me. I await (as you are able) your response.

Greg L. Price

A Letter Responding to Argument #4 (1 Corinthians 11:7-9)

May 7, 2011

THE FOURTH ARGUMENT FROM 1 CORINTHIANS 11:7-9

Dear ___,

Thank you for your continued encouragement and responses in working through the 8 Arguments which you submitted to me at the outset of our study through 1 Corinthians 11:2-16. I move now to your 4th Argument which is taken from 1 Corinthians 11:7-9 wherein you state:

> 4. Paul's instructions that a man not cover his head because he is made in the 'image of God', cannot be cultural, for man is always in the image of God (vss. 7-9) [from your email dated 1/20/11—GLP].

Before continuing with my response, I want to make it clear that when addressing male headship, the Scripture (nor myself) intends to communicate a headship devoid of love and care for the women under that headship. In fact, the supreme example of loving and caring headship is that of Christ who laid down His own life to save and rescue His bride (Ephesians 5:25-28). Any other kind of headship than a self-sacrificial headship that mirrors (though imperfectly) the headship of Christ is not a biblical concept of headship. Though headship communicates the idea of superior rank, it does not communicate the idea of cruel and abusive treatment of those who hold an inferior rank. In fact, men who hold the superior rank are especially to give honor to women who hold the inferior rank (1 Peter 3:7). Rather than beating women down, men are to prize, protect, and exalt women as serving the very purpose of God just as men serve the purpose of God, each in their respective roles. Therefore, all that has been said (and all that shall be said) in respect to the headship of men and the submission of women should be continually understood within these biblical parameters.

Up to this point (1 Corinthians 11:3-6), Paul has argued for the headship of man and the submission of woman from the MORAL/THEOLOGICAL principles of headship and submission found in 1 Corinthians 11:3; he then applies these MORAL/THEOLOGICAL principles of headship and submission to a very specific instance of abuse in 1 Corinthians 11:4-6. Because "the head of the woman is the man" (1 Corinthians 11:3), Christians in Corinth who met together for worship were to appear in the cultural and customary signs (recognized within Corinth) of man's headship (namely, the uncovered head) and of woman's submission (namely, the covered head). When a Christian woman in Corinth removed the outward customary sign of submission (the covered head) as she entered the Christian assembly, she usurped the role of man (generically all men, and particularly the role of her own father and/or husband), she brought shame upon man (generically upon all men, and particularly upon her own father and/or husband) as the Divinely appointed head over the woman (which likewise was an indirect attack upon God Himself who established the headship of man and the submission of woman from the beginning of creation). Having laid one piece of the foundation of his argument (and having applied it as well to a specific case in the Church of Corinth), Paul is now ready to lay another piece of the foundation of his argument in addressing the problem in the Church of Corinth.

Moving from the MORAL/THEOLOGICAL principles of headship and submission found in 1 Corinthians 11:3, Paul now lays the next piece of the foundation of his argument in addressing the confusion and schism brought into the Church of Corinth by men *possibly* covering themselves and by women *actually* uncovering themselves: man is the image and glory of God (1 Corinthians 11:7).

First, Paul begins this verse with "for" (*gar* in Greek) so as to provide a supporting argument to that of 1 Corinthians 11:3 in explaining on the one hand why Christian men in Corinth ought not to cover their heads when they assemble for worship, and on the other hand why Christian women ought to keep their heads covered when they assemble for worship. Just as Paul began with the men (in 1 Corinthians 11:4) and then proceeded to the women (in 1 Corinthians 11:5,6), so likewise Paul follows the same course here in laying the second piece of his foundation: first, he specifically mentions the men (in 1 Corinthians 11:7: "For a man indeed ought not to cover his head"); second, he specifically mentions the women (in 1 Corinthians 11:10: "For this cause ought the woman to have power on her head").

Second, whereas in 1 Corinthians 11:3-6, Paul began by

laying the foundation (in 1 Corinthians 11:3), and then proceeded to the cultural application within the Christian assembly (in 1 Corinthians 11:4-6), here in 1 Corinthians 11:7a, Paul reverses that order and begins with the cultural application to men within the Christian assembly ("For a man indeed ought not to cover his head"), and then lays the foundation afterward in 1 Corinthians 11:7b-9, after which he returns with the cultural application to women within the Christian assembly (1 Corinthians 11:10).

Third, the cultural application to men within the Christian assembly is simply stated that "a man indeed ought not to cover his head" (1 Corinthians 11:7), which is in essence restating what Paul declared in 1 Corinthians 11:4. However, there is a certain "oughtness" stated by Paul in this application to men ("a man indeed OUGHT NOT to cover his head"). Does this imply that an uncovered head for men is a universal moral duty in all cultural and/or ecclesiastical contexts? I submit that such is neither a good nor a necessary inference to draw from Paul's words. For there is likewise an "oughtness" by way of command associated with other cultural practices in Scripture that are not universal moral duties to all subsequent generations, nations, or churches on earth: (1) the Divine prohibition against cutting the corner of the beard was a cultural practice forbidden to the Israelites because it mimicked the practices of Canaanite religions (Leviticus 19:27), and therefore not a universal moral prohibition; (2) the Divine command to shave the head so as to become bald was a cultural practice of ancient times signifying grief and shame (Micah 1:16), but it is not a universal moral duty; (3) the Divine charge to put on sackcloth was a cultural practice of ancient times also signifying grief and shame (Jeremiah 6:26), but it is not a universal moral duty; (4) the authorization by Christ for

His disciples to wash the feet of one another (using the same Greek word for "ought" as is used in 1 Corinthians 11:7) was a cultural practice of ancient times signifying loving service (John 13:14), but it is not a universal moral duty; and (5) the apostolic imperative to greet one another with a holy kiss was a cultural practice of ancient times signifying friendship and fellowship (Romans 16:16; 1 Corinthians 16:20; 2 Corinthians 13:12; 1 Thessalonians 5:26), but is not a universal moral duty. Thus, we see that a Divine prohibition, a Divine command, or a Divine "oughtness" does not a universal moral duty necessarily make. For if the "oughtness" of Christ in regard to washing the feet of one another ("If then, your Lord and Master, have washed your feet; ye OUGHT to wash one another's feet" John 13:14) does not necessarily infer a universal moral duty binding all Christians and all churches in all ages of the world (I assume at this point and will not argue further that you do not believe that foot-washing is a universal moral command binding all Christians and all churches in all ages), then the "oughtness" of Paul in regard to men not covering their heads in public worship ("For a man indeed OUGHT not to cover his head" 1 Corinthians 11:7) does not necessarily infer a universal moral duty binding all Christians and all churches in all ages of the world. Therefore, I submit the "oughtness" of Paul's words in 1 Corinthians 11:7 ("For a man indeed OUGHT not to cover his head") is not a MORAL "oughtness", but rather a CULTURAL "oughtness" demanded by Paul so as to avoid shame, gender confusion, and ecclesiastical schism within the Church of Corinth.

Fourth, the reason given why the man in that cultural context of Corinth was not to put on a headcovering when he gathered for the public worship of God is stated by Paul as follows: "forasmuch as he is the image and glory of God" (1 Corinthians 11:7). Two questions now arise: (1) How is man the IMAGE of God in distinction to woman? (2) How is man the GLORY of God in distinction to woman?

1st. How is man the IMAGE of God in distinction to woman?

According to the biblical account found in Genesis 1:26,27, both male and female were created in the image of God. So why did Paul apply "image" only to the man here in 1 Corinthians 11:7? Just as Paul previously focused narrowly on Christ being the head of every man (1 Corinthians 11:3), even though it is generally true that Christ is the head of every woman as well; so Paul likewise here in 1 Corinthians 11:7 focuses narrowly on man being the image of God, even though it is generally true that woman is the image of God as well. The reason it would appear for Paul narrowing the focus upon man in 1 Corinthians 11:3 and in 1 Corinthians 11:7 is due to the headship that is unique to man (in relation to the woman) in reflecting the sovereignty of Christ and God over all creation. Although both man and woman are made in the image of God in knowledge, in righteousness, in holiness, and in dominion over the creatures, man (in distinction to woman) more narrowly reflects Christ's and God's lordship and headship in that man is the head of the woman by God's appointment (as already stated in 1 Corinthians 11:3, "the head of the woman is the man", and as will be further demonstrated in what follows in 1 Corinthians 11:8,9). Thus, the image of God (as to ROLE not NATURE) is manifested in the man by way of God's appointment from the time of creation that the head of the woman is the man. When addressing the NATURE of man and woman, both are made in the image of God. When addressing the ROLE of man and woman, man is the image of God because man is Divinely ordained to be the head of the woman (as Paul will make clear in 1 Corinthians 11:8,9).

2nd. How is man the GLORY of God in distinction to woman?

Once again, it would be perfectly appropriate and biblical to speak of both man and woman being the glory of God when speaking of them as to their nature and essence. Since both were made in the image of God, both are meant to reflect the glory of God. But since Paul is not here addressing man and woman as to NATURE, but is rather addressing man and woman as to ROLE, what was said above in regard to man being in a narrow sense "the image of God" in relationship to his headship over woman, so likewise it is said here in regard to man being in a narrow sense "the glory of God" in relationship to his headship over woman. Man is the glory of God (in distinction to woman) because he has been divinely ordained to reflect God's headship in his headship over the woman. Man's headship is intended to bring honor to God as the Sovereign of all creation. In other words, the headship of man is intended to reflect the glory that supremely belongs to the Most High God who created all things for His own glory. This truth lays a great responsibility upon every man; for every man is duty bound to exercise his headship not to please himself, but rather to please God who appointed to man the rank of head over the woman. Because man is responsible to exercise his headship in honor, in love, and to the glory of God, man will also be judged accordingly on the Last Day. Headship is, therefore, not to be treated lightly or to engender pride, but rather ought to humble every man in reverently reflecting to women the just and benevolent headship of God.

Fifth, Paul lays the second piece of his foundation in declaring that a man ought not to cover his head (a cultural and customary sign of female submission), since man is particularly the image and glory of God (in distinction to woman). The first piece of Paul's foundation having been laid (i.e. the MORAL/THEOLOGICAL principle that "the head of the woman is the man" 1 Corinthians 11:3), the second piece of Paul's foundation is now laid (i.e. the CREATION ORDINANCE that man "is the image and glory of God" 1 Corinthians 11:7). It must once again be noted that it is NEITHER the uncovered head itself NOR the covered head itself that is the CREATION ORDINANCE established by God, but rather the CREATION ORDINANCE established by God is that man "is the image and glory of God" (1 Corinthians 11:7) in his headship over woman, and (as we shall next observe) that "woman is the glory of man" (1 Corinthians 11:7) in her submission to man. Confusing the cultural and customary sign with the CREATION ORDINANCE will inevitably lead to the wrong conclusion. Paul identifies the CREATION ORDINANCE established by God (man as the image and glory of God, and woman as the glory of man) so as to instruct the Corinthian Christians that those cultural and customary signs (like the uncovered head of men and the covered head of women) which reflect the CREATION ORDINANCE ought not to be disregarded or cast off when assembling within the Church of Corinth to worship the Lord.

Sixth, we will return to the woman being the glory of the man as we consider your Fifth Argument. But for the present (as we are considering your Fourth Argument), let us briefly consider how Paul proves from Scripture that man is "the image and glory of God". Paul uses two arguments from the creation account to confirm that "man is the image and glory of God".

1ˢᵗ. Man was created first (i.e. before woman) by God from the dust of the ground: "**For the man is not of the woman**; but the woman of the man" (1 Corinthians 11:8). Man did not have his origin from woman, but woman had her origin from man: (1) "And the LORD God formed man of the dust of the ground, and breathed into his nostrils the breath of life; and man became a living soul" (Genesis 2:7); (2) "And the rib, which the LORD God had taken from man, made he a woman, and brought her unto the man" (Genesis 2:22). Man and woman were not created simultaneously as if they were equal in headship. Nor was woman created before man and man created from woman as if woman was the head of man. Thus, because man was created first by God (and was created by God independent of the woman), and because woman was created from the man, Paul argues that man is "the image and glory of God" reflecting the headship of God over His creation.

2ⁿᵈ. Man was not created for the woman since the woman did not exist when man was created by God: "**Neither was the man created for the woman**; but the woman for the man" (1 Corinthians 11:9). After the man was created by God, it became apparent to the man that he did not have a mate corresponding to him as did the animals that he had named. God declares, "It is not good that the man should be alone; I will make him a help meet for him" (Genesis 2:18). Thus, because the man was not created by God to be a woman's helper (but the woman to be the man's helper), man was created to be the head of the woman; and Paul, therefore, argues that man is "the image and glory of God" reflecting the headship of God over His creation. These two arguments in 1 Corinthians 11:8,9 thus provide Paul biblical warrant for why man (in distinction to woman) is "the image and glory of God".

Seventh, thus, ____, when you state, "Paul's instructions that a man not cover his head because he is made in the 'image of God', cannot be cultural, for man is always in the image of God", you are absolutely right! Man being "the image and glory of God" is not cultural; it is a CREATION ORDINANCE that applies to all men, in all cultures, in all churches, and in all ages (as Paul demonstrates in 1 Corinthians 11:8,9). However, the uncovered head of men (and the covered head of women) in the society of Corinth or in the Church of Corinth was cultural (and not a CREATION ORDINANCE). For it is clear from the scriptural account of creation and of the fall that both the man and the woman were created with uncovered heads, worshipped in the Garden with uncovered heads, and fell with uncovered heads — there was no distinction between the outward appearance of the man and the outward appearance of the woman with regard to the headcovering. Thus, the CREATION ORDINANCE was not the uncovered head of man vs. the covered head of woman, but was rather the headship of man as "the image and glory of God" vs. the submission of woman as "the glory of man".

A Letter Responding to Argument #5 (1 Corinthians 11:7-9)

May 7, 2011

THE FIFTH ARGUMENT FROM 1 CORINTHIANS 11:7-9

___, I now consider your Fifth Argument which you have stated as follows:

> 5. Similarly, the woman perpetually wears a headcovering because she is always in the 'image of man'. (vs. 7). (see also at this point that a woman ought to have her head covered 'because of the angels' v. 10) [from your email dated 1/20/11—GLP].

This summary of where we are in Paul's argument is the same summary provided under the Fourth Argument. Up to this point (1 Corinthians 11:3-6), Paul has argued for the headship of man and the submission of woman from the MORAL/THEOLOGICAL principles of headship and submission found in 1 Corinthians 11:3; he then applies these MORAL/THEOLOGICAL principles of headship and submission to a very specific instance of abuse in 1 Corinthians 11:4-6. Because "the head of the woman is the man" (1 Corinthians 11:3), Christians in Corinth who met together for worship were to appear in the cultural and customary signs (recognized within Corinth) of man's headship (namely, the uncovered head) and of woman's submission (namely, the covered head). When a Christian woman in Corinth removed the outward customary sign of submission (the covered head) as she entered the Christian assembly, she usurped the role of man (generically all men, and particularly the role of her own father and/or husband), she brought shame upon man (generically upon all men, and particularly upon her own father and/or husband) as the Divinely appointed head over the woman (which likewise was an indirect attack upon God Himself who established the headship of man and the submission of woman from the beginning of creation). Having laid one piece of the foundation of his argument (and having applied it as well to a specific case in the Church of Corinth), Paul is now ready to lay another piece of the foundation of his argument in addressing the problem in the Church of Corinth.

Moving from the MORAL/THEOLOGICAL principles of headship and submission found in 1 Corinthians 11:3 (and the cultural application of those principles in 1 Corinthians 11:4-6), Paul now lays the next piece of the foundation of his argument in addressing the confusion and schism brought into the Church of Corinth by men *possibly* covering themselves and by women *actually* uncovering themselves: "the woman is the glory of the man" (1 Corinthians 11:7). This is the opposite side of the same coin in laying the foundation of his second argument — an argument taken from a CREATION ORDINANCE. Whereas this CREATION ORDINANCE demonstrates on the one hand that man is "the image and glory of God" (1 Corinthians 11:7), this same CREATION ORDINANCE also demonstrates on the other hand that woman is "the glory of the man" (1 Corinthians 11:7).

First, whereas Paul began with the specific cultural appli-

83

cation to men within the Christian assembly ("For a man indeed ought not to cover his head" 1 Corinthians 11:7) and then proceeded to lay the second piece of the foundation (namely, that of a CREATION ORDINANCE) to his argument ("forasmuch as he is the image and glory of God" 1 Corinthians 11:7), Paul now reverses that order as he addresses women, and begins with the second piece of the foundation (namely, that of a CREATION ORDINANCE) to his argument ("but the woman is the glory of the man" 1 Corinthians 11:7), and then proceeds to the cultural application to women within the Christian assembly ("For this cause ought the woman to have power on her head because of the angels" 1 Corinthians 11:10). This I submit by way of an overview of how Paul presents his argument.

Second, The "but" (*de* in Greek) that begins this part of the sentence ("BUT the woman is the glory of the man" 1 Corinthians 11:7) conveys a contrast with what was just stated by Paul. On the one hand, "man is the image and glory of God", "but" on the other hand, "woman is the glory of man." Since the reason that Paul uses the word "image [of God]" in regard to man is in order to convey the idea that man (in distinction to woman) bears God's image of headship and authority (as to ROLE not NATURE), it would be inappropriate (if not incorrect) to speak of woman being the "image" of man (in as much as "image" in this context relates to the ROLE of headship bestowed upon man as a creation ordinance). Thus, it is important to note, ___, that Paul does not state that woman is the "image of man" (contrary to what you have stated in your Fifth Argument, "the woman perpetually wears a headcovering **because she is always in the 'image of man'**"), but rather that she is the "glory of man". Moreover, when you state in your Fifth Argument that "the woman PERPETUALLY wears a headcovering be-

cause she is always in the 'image of man'", the inference
that I draw from such a statement is that a woman ought
to wear a headcovering in all public contexts (not simply
ecclesiastical contexts) because she is "the glory of man"
not only when she assembles for the public worship of
God, but also whenever she appears in public. I would
submit that your Fifth Argument does not (and cannot)
argue for a woman wearing a headcovering only in public worship (and not in public society in general). Thus,
____, your Fifth Argument actually proves too much and
argues that women ought to be covered in public at all
times (both in civil society and ecclesiastical society).

Third, how is woman "the glory of man" (as stated by
Paul in 1 Corinthians 11:7)? As I stated earlier in my response to the Fourth Argument (when discussing how
man is "the glory of God"), it would be perfectly appropriate and biblical to speak of both man and woman
being the glory of God when speaking of them as to their
NATURE and ESSENCE. Since both were made in the
image of God (as to NATURE, Genesis 1:26,27), both are
meant to reflect the glory of God. But since Paul (in the
context of 1 Corinthians 11:7-9) is not here addressing
man and woman as to NATURE, but is rather addressing man and woman as to ROLE, just as we must understand man as "the glory of God" to relate to the ROLE
of man (in distinction to that of the ROLE of woman), so
we must likewise understand woman as "the glory of
man" to relate to the ROLE of woman (in distinction to
that of the ROLE of man). Woman is "the glory of man"
(in distinction to man being "the glory of God") because
she has been divinely ordained to reflect the glory of the
man in submitting to man's headship over her. Woman is
as Calvin puts it, "a distinguished ornament of the man;
for it is a great honour that God has appointed her to the
man as the partner of his life, and a helper to him, and

has made her subject to him as the body is to the head" (see Calvin's Commentary on 1 Corinthians 11:7, Baker Book House, p. 357). Woman is the most brilliant jewel in a man's crown, and for that reason she is to be loved, cherished, and honored in her ROLE of submission to the man, and not despised, demeaned, or dishonored. Woman as "the glory of man" is not to be trodden under foot, but rather is to be exalted as a helper to the very side and heart of man. Not only will man stand before God on the Last Day to answer for how he honored woman as a fit helper to him ordained by God, but woman will also stand before God on the Last Day to answer for how she brought glory to man in his ROLE as head over her. Some women no doubt have ground to complain of the abuse and tyranny exercised by men in their lives, but the abuse and tyranny of some does not alter the universal CREATION ORDINANCE established by God. The response of a faithful woman in such a case of physical abuse and tyranny is not to cast off the CREATION ORDINANCE (namely, that she is "the glory of the man") established by God, but is rather to flee (if necessary for physical safety) the physical abuse of particular men (as required by the Sixth Commandment to preserve both our own life and the life of others), while still acknowledging the CREATION ORDINANCE (namely, that she as a woman is still intended by God to be the glory of man). Both the church and state ought to deal with physical abuse in a marriage (whether it comes from the man or whether it comes from the woman).

Fourth, Paul next (in 1 Corinthians 11:8,9) sets out to prove from the Scripture not only that "man is the image and glory of God", but also that "the woman is the glory of man". We previously had opportunity to review Paul's biblical proof (as referenced in 1 Corinthians 11:8,9) that "man is the image and glory of God." Now we will observe Paul's biblical warrant (as likewise referenced in 1 Corinthians 11:8,9) that "woman is the glory of man". For the same biblical references alluded to in 1 Corinthians 11:8,9 both prove that "man is the image and glory of God" and that "woman is the glory of man", as we shall see. There are two biblical proofs from the creation account alluded to by Paul that demonstrate that "woman is the glory of man".

1st. Woman was created by God after man and had her origin from the rib of man: "For the man is not of the woman; **but the woman of the man**" (1 Corinthians 11:8). The Old Testament passage that Paul alludes to is the following: "And the rib, which the LORD God had taken from man, made he a woman, and brought her unto the man" (Genesis 2:22). Thus, because woman was created AFTER man and was created FROM man (dependent upon man for her creation as ordained by God), Paul argues that "woman is the glory of man" and should reflect man's glory as her head by means of her willing submission.

2nd. Woman was created by God to be a helper to man: "Neither was the man created for the woman; **but the woman for the man**" (1 Corinthians 11:9). As man was first created by God, he did not have a mate who could help him propagate the race and help him in his calling. God saw the condition of man being alone as "not good": "It is not good that the man should be alone; I will make him a help meet for him" (Genesis 2:18). Thus, for this reason was woman created by God—to be man's helper (to submit to him, not to rule over him), and in that ROLE "woman is the glory of man", the most brilliant jewel in his crown. These two arguments in 1 Corinthians 11:8,9 thus provide Paul biblical warrant for why woman (as to her God-ordained ROLE, not as to her NATURE or

ESSENCE) is "the glory of man."

Fifth, once again, it bears repeating that Paul does not argue that the headcovering is a creation ordinance for woman, for nothing alluded to by Paul in 1 Corinthians 11:8,9 indicates that Eve was given a headcovering to wear in the Garden of Eden for worship or otherwise. What Paul argues to be a CREATION ORDINANCE established by God in regard to the woman is that she was created by God to be "the glory of man." Thus, the CREATION ORDINANCE established by God and argued by Paul in 1 Corinthians 11:7-9 is NOT the headcovering, but rather is woman created to be "the glory of man" (as to her ROLE). The headcovering is the cultural and customary sign; woman created to be "the glory of man" is the CREATION ORDINANCE. The cultural and customary sign may vary from culture to culture, from church to church, or from age to age; but the CREATION ORDINANCE can never vary from culture to culture, from church to church nor from age to age.

Sixth, Paul now proceeds to give the cultural application within the Christian assembly of this CREATION ORDINANCE (namely, that "woman is the glory of man" 1 Corinthians 11:7) in 1 Corinthians 11:10: "For this cause ought the woman to have power on her head because of the angels." Does the prepositional phrase ("For this cause") that introduces this sentence refer back to the CREATION ORDINANCE (namely, that "woman is the glory of man" in 1 Corinthians 11:7 and to the biblical proofs alluded to in the creation account in 1 Corinthians 11:8,9), or does the prepositional phrase ("For this cause") that introduces this sentence refer forward to the prepositional phrase at the end of 1 Corinthians 11:10: "because of the angels." In other words, is Paul teaching that the reason for a woman to have power on her head is because she is "the glory of man" (1 Corinthians 11:7-9), or "because of the angels" (1 Corinthians 11:10). I would submit that it is unnecessary to make this an either/or exegetical decision (i.e. the reason for a woman to have power on her head is EITHER because she is "the glory of man" OR "because of the angels"), but rather one may make this a both/and exegetical decision (i.e. the reason for a woman to have power on her head is BOTH because she is "the glory of man" AND "because of the angels"). Thus, I submit that the propositional phrase ("For this cause") that introduces this sentence refers BOTH backward AND forward.

1ˢᵗ. Thus, the first cause and reason why the woman ought to have power on her head (1 Corinthians 11:10) is because she is "the glory of man" (1 Corinthians 11:7) in reflecting (by means of her submission) his headship. Once again, Paul uses the word "ought" in regard to the Christian woman in Corinth having power on her head (which is the same Greek word used by Paul in 1 Corinthians 11:7 in regard to the man being uncovered). The "oughtness" referenced here by Paul in regard to the Christian woman within the Corinthian Church having power on her head (1 Corinthians 11:10) is parallel to the "oughtness" referenced earlier by Paul in regard to the Christian man within the Corinthian Church being uncovered (1 Corinthians 11:7). I would suggest that what was said above under the Fourth Argument be reviewed. But especially it should be remembered that if the "oughtness" of Christ in regard to washing the feet of one another ("If then, your Lord and Master, have washed your feet; ye OUGHT to wash one another's feet" John 13:14) does not necessarily infer a universal moral duty binding all Christians in all churches in all ages of the world, then the "oughtness" of Paul in regard to women having power on their heads in public worship

("For this cause OUGHT the woman to have power on her head because of the angels" 1 Corinthians 11:10) does not necessarily infer a universal moral duty binding all Christian women in all churches in all ages of the world. Therefore, the "oughtness" of Paul's words in 1 Corinthians 11:10 ("For this cause OUGHT the woman to have power on her head") is not a MORAL "oughtness", but is rather a CULTURAL "oughtness", which is demanded by Paul so as to avoid shame, gender confusion, and ecclesiastical schism within the Church of Corinth.

But what does Paul mean when he demands that "the woman ought to have POWER on her head"? What is the "power" that the woman is to have on her head? Since the whole context of 1 Corinthians 11:3-16 has in view a particular ecclesiastical case wherein women in the Church of Corinth were removing their headcoverings when they assembled for the public worship of God, it would be most natural to the context to identify the "power" on the head of a woman as the fabric headcovering (note Paul's disapproval of a woman being uncovered in 1 Corinthians 11:5; Paul's command given to the woman to have her head covered in 1 Corinthians 11:6; and the uncomeliness Paul associated with a woman who prays with her head uncovered in 1 Corinthians 11:13). Thus, if anything is to be placed "on the head" of the Christian woman in Corinth when she assembled for the public worship of God, the entire context of this passage expects that the reader would understand that to be a fabric headcovering. Hence, the context of this passage should naturally guide us to interpret the "power" on the head of the Christian woman in Corinth to be a fabric headcovering.

But didn't the headcovering signify in Corinth at that time a woman's submission rather than her power or her authority? Yes, this is true. However, what Paul means in this instance is NOT that the headcovering on the head of the Christian woman in Corinth is her own power and authority to exercise over herself or over the man, but rather that the headcovering on the head of the Christian woman in Corinth is a token of her submission to the power and authority of the man. To introduce at this point a woman's power, authority, and headship would be completely contrary to all that Paul has stated (especially in 1 Corinthians 11:3,5,6,7,8,9). Thus, the context demands that the power, authority, and headship belong to the man and that "the woman ought to have power on her head", in showing by the cultural token of a headcovering, her willing submission to the power, authority, and headship of man. This use of the word "power" as representing the cultural token of female submission (i.e. the headcovering) to a man's power is an instance of a figure of speech called metonymy. Metonymy is used often in Scripture when either an object is used to represent an idea (e.g. "key" which is an object, represents power to open and close which is an idea, in Isaiah 22:22 and Matthew 16:19), or vice versa, an idea is used to represent an object (e.g. "covenant" which is a theological idea, represents circumcision which is an object, in Genesis 17:13; or as in the present case, "power" which is an idea, is used to represent the headcovering which is an object and token of submission to power). Thus, in summary, Paul first states there is a cultural "oughtness" for a Christian woman in Corinth to have power (i.e. a headcovering) on her head (1 Corinthians 11:10), namely, because she is "the glory of the man" (1 Corinthians 11:7). But there is a second reason given by Paul.

2nd. The second cause and reason why the Christian woman within the Corinthian Church ought to have power on her head (1 Corinthians 11:10) is "because of the angels" (1 Corinthians 11:10). ___, although you did not spell it out as a separate and distinct Argument, you imply that the prepositional phrase ("because of the angels" 1 Corinthians 11:10) provides another Argument for the non-cultural nature of the headcovering in 1 Corinthians chapter 11: "(see also at this point that a woman ought to have her head covered 'because of the angels' v. 10)." I agree that Paul uses the angels here as another reason why the Christian women in Corinth ought to cover their heads in the public worship of God. However, I do not agree that "the angels" proves or implies that Christian women in all churches and in all ages throughout the world (without exception) ought to cover their heads in the public worship of God. I understand the angels to refer to the elect angels of God. The elect angels of God are sent as ministering spirits to minister to the heirs of salvation (Hebrews 1:14). Moreover, the Lord Jesus implies (in Matthew 18:10) that all of God's children have holy angels who particularly care for them (as "their angels"). Finally, I would mention that the holy angels of God witness our religious acts of worship in oaths as indicated by Paul (1 Timothy 3:16). Because the holy angels of God are sent to minister to God's people, to protect them, and to witness their acts of worship, it stands to reason that the holy angels of God can also be grieved by the sin of God's people, by their errors, and by their bringing confusion and schism into the public worship of God. In the particular case addressed by Paul here in 1 Corinthians 11, since the uncovered head of the man was a cultural token of male headship and the covered head of the woman was a cultural token of female submission, when the Christian woman entered the public worship of God and removed the cultural token of her submission to man, she brought shame upon man who was her head (and ultimately upon God who ordained the headship of man over woman), but such gender confusion and schism in the Christian assembly also grieved the holy angels of God who witnessed such perversion of the role of women by Christian women in Corinth. Thus, the second cause and reason why the Christian woman in Corinth ought to continue to have a headcovering on her head (rather than removing it) when passing from civil society into the public worship of God was on account of the sorrow brought to God's ministering spirits (the holy angels of God).

It should be observed that if "the angels" provide a just reason why Christian women in the Church of Corinth ought to be covered in the public worship of God, then "the angels" also provide a just reason why Christian women in the Church of Corinth ought to be covered in public civil society as well. For "the angels" not only were grieved by gender confusion and role reversal in Christian women when they gathered for public worship in Corinth, but also were grieved by gender confusion and role reversal in Christian women when they gathered for any public meeting in civil society. For "the angels" were not limited or confined to ministering to Christian women, protecting Christian women, and witnessing the acts of Christian women in Corinth only when they gathered for the public worship of God. Their ministry, protection, and bearing witness extended to all occasions in public society. Thus, Paul's reason ("because of the angels") for a Christian woman in Corinth to be covered both infers that the headcovering was worn in Corinth by Christian women not only in the public worship of God, but also was generally worn in Corinth by Christian women in public civil society as well, and also infers that the headcovering that was worn in Corinth by Christian women in public society was being removed when they entered into the public worship of God (thus bringing shame, gender confusion, and schism into the ecclesiastical society and providing the specific occasion for Paul addressing the problem within the Church of Corinth).

The prepositional phrase ("because of the angels") does not infer that the covered head of a woman is a universal moral requirement, it only infers that "the angels" are always grieved by disorder and confusion (i.e. when the general moral principles of order and decorum are violated) in the respective roles of men and women (particularly among Christians in the public worship of God). Since the headship of men and the submission of women are a CREATION ORDINANCE, "the angels" would always be grieved by a Christian woman who exchanges the cultural and customary sign of her female submission for the cultural and customary sign of male headship. Such perverse actions on the part of Christian men or Christian women disrupt the order and decorum established by God ("For God is not the author of confusion, but of peace" 1 Corinthians 14:33; "Let all things be done decently and in order" 1 Corinthians 14:40). Thus, there is no inconsistency or contradiction in Paul maintaining that the headcovering was a cultural and customary sign of female submission and yet maintaining that the angels of God (who are not limited to a particular culture or age) are grieved by Christian women who lay aside the cultural and customary sign of female submission in Corinth (i.e. the covered head) and take upon themselves the cultural and customary sign of male headship in Corinth (i.e. the uncovered head).

Seventh, Paul takes occasion in 1 Corinthians 11:11,12 before closing this part of his argument to provide a proper balance to what he had just said in regard to the woman being the glory of the man (1 Corinthians 11:7), having her origin from man (1 Corinthians 11:8), and being created in order to be a man's helper (1 Corinthians 11:9). Paul has duly corrected those Christian women in Corinth who had assumed the cultural role of a man in the public worship of God, but now he points out that there is also a sense in which the man is not independent of the woman or the woman independent of the man in the Lord (1 Corinthians 11:11). As to Christian grace in the faith of our Lord Jesus Christ, Christian men and Christian women are dependent upon one another, for they are "heirs together of the grace of life" (1 Peter 3:7). Paul provides a further explanation of how men and women are dependent upon one another (in 1 Corinthians 11:12) when he teaches that just as the woman was originally created from the man, so now the man is born of the woman (all by the will of God and to the glory of God).

___, I have now covered in this installment your Fourth and Fifth Arguments. Please feel free to follow-up with any questions or comments that might arise from my responses.

Yours for the Cause of Christ,
Greg L. Price

A Letter Responding to Argument #6 (1 Corinthians 11:13)

June 10, 2011

THE SIXTH ARGUMENT FROM 1 CORINTHIANS 11:13

Dear ___, although this has been a long process in addressing the Arguments you have presented for the perpetual ecclesiastical use of headcoverings for women in the public worship of God, it has allowed us to think, meditate, study, and pray as we have considered what the Holy Spirit is saying through His inspired apostle in 1 Corinthians 11. The time we have spent over the past few months has been most helpful to me in preparing my exegetical/theological remarks to each of your Arguments. Thank you for your willingness and desire to take this journey with me. I do appreciate it very much.

We come now to your Sixth Argument which you have stated as follows:

> 6. In v. 13 he appeals to the conscience, governed by the perpetual moral law, of the Corinthians as a reason to persist in the ordinance of v. 2. (vs. 13)" [from your email dated 1/20/11 – GLP].

___, we have previously noted that Paul has now laid

two distinct pieces of the foundation to his argument in addressing the particular abuse reported to him within the Corinthian Church. (1) The first piece of the foundation of Paul's argument is the argument from MORAL/ THEOLOGICAL principles of headship and submission found in 1 Corinthians 11:3: "the head of the woman is the man." These MORAL/THEOLOGICAL principles of headship and submission are then applied to the confusion and schism within the Corinthian Church in 1 Corinthians 11:4-6. (2) The second piece of the foundation of Paul's argument is the argument from CREATION ORDINANCES in 1 Corinthians 11:7: "he [i.e. man — GLP] is the image and glory of God; but the woman is the glory of the man." These CREATION ORDINANCES are further demonstrated in 1 Corinthians 11:8,9, and then are applied to the confusion and schism within the Corinthian Church in 1 Corinthians 11:7 ("For a man indeed ought not to cover his head") and in 1 Corinthians 11:10 ("For this cause ought the woman to have power on her head"). This now brings us to the third piece of the foundation to Paul's argument: an argument from PROPRIETY AND DECORUM in 1 Corinthians 11:13 ("Judge in yourselves: is it comely that a woman pray unto God uncovered?").

First, Paul begins with a command to the members of the Corinthian Church: "Judge in yourselves" (1 Corinthians 11:13). I take Paul's command here not as an appeal to each member's conscience in Corinth, as if he were saying, "Each one of you judge for yourself within your own individual conscience." Rather, I submit that Paul's appeal in this command is an appeal to the church collectively in Corinth to come together and decide (the Greek word, *krino*, may be translated here in this verse as "decide" according to the standard Greek lexicon entitled, *A Greek-English Lexicon Of The New Testament And*

Other Early Christian Literature by Bauer, Arndt, Gingrich, p. 452) among yourselves what is fitting in this case of a woman praying uncovered in the public worship of God. In other words, I would submit that the following literal translation makes clearer the inspired intention of Paul: "Decide among you yourselves [the use of "yourselves" here is the intensive use of the Greek pronoun, *autois* — GLP]." Paul uses a propositional phrase after the command ("judge"), which the Authorized Version translates as "in yourselves" (*en humin* in the Greek text). Does this prepositional phrase, "in yourselves" (*en humin*), mean that the Corinthian Christians are to personally judge within their own individual consciences, or does it mean that they are to judge (or decide) among the themselves collectively when the Church of Corinth comes together? The instances of Paul's use of the Greek prepositional phrase (*en humin*) to mean, "among you" collectively as a group or as a church (rather than "in you" individually as distinctive persons) in the Letter of 1 Corinthians are numerous: 1 Corinthians 1:6,10,11; 2:2; 3:3,16,18; 5:1; 6:5; 11:13,18, 19 (2 times in verse 19),30; 14:25; 15:12. The only instances of the Greek prepositional phrase (*en humin*) in the entire Letter of 1 Corinthians in which the context makes it clear that it could not mean "among you" collectively as a group or as a church are found in 1 Corinthians 6:2 where *en humin* means "by you", and in 1 Corinthians 6:19 where *en humin* means "in you" individually (that is, "within your individual physical body"). Thus, it seems far more likely that when Paul issues his command in 1 Corinthians 11:13 ("Judge in yourselves"), he means to say in effect, "Decide **among you yourselves** when you come together, is it comely that a woman pray unto God uncovered?"

Thus, ___, if the translation above reflects accurately the intention of the Holy Spirit (which the common use of

98

the prepositional phrase in question decidedly favors in 1 Corinthians), there is NOT a direct appeal by Paul to the individual conscience of each person in the Church of Corinth to personally judge for himself/herself whether a woman praying with an uncovered head violates the Moral Law of God. On the contrary, the evidence would support the view that Paul's command is an appeal for the Church of Corinth to come together collectively in order to discuss and to decide whether it is fitting and proper for a woman to remove the cultural and customary sign of female submission when she assembles with the church to worship the Lord.

Second, in the second part of 1 Corinthians 11:13, Paul reveals in the form of a question what it is that the Corinthian Church collectively is to decide among itself when it comes together: "Is it comely that a woman pray unto God uncovered?" Carefully note that Paul doesn't ask, "Is it MORALLY LAWFUL (or is it LAWFUL ACCORDING TO THE REGULATIVE PRINCIPLE OF WORSHIP) that a woman pray unto God uncovered?" Paul under inspiration of the Holy Spirit chooses a Greek participle (*prepon*) that means "be fitting, be seemly or suitable" (according to *A Greek-English Lexicon Of The New Testament And Other Early Christian Literature* by Bauer, Arndt, Gingrich, p.706). Thus, Paul is not asking the Church of Corinth to decide whether a woman who prays unto God uncovered has violated the Moral Law of God or the Regulative Principle of Worship. But rather Paul appeals to the Church of Corinth to decide whether it is fitting and suitable for a Christian woman in Corinth to exchange the cultural and customary sign of female submission (i.e. the covered head) for the cultural and customary sign of male headship (i.e. the uncovered head). Moreover, the standard of whether it was fitting and suitable for a Christian woman in Corinth to remove her headcovering (which she was wearing in civil society prior to entering worship) is not stated to be the Moral Law of God, but rather NATURE (1 Corinthians 11:14). Paul declares that NATURE teaches the Corinthians whether it is fitting or suitable for a Christian woman to pray with the cultural and customary sign of male headship (i.e. the uncovered head), for NATURE itself teaches there are to be distinctive roles and appearances between men and women. As we shall see NATURE neither teaches that all men in all cultures, in all nations, and in all ages ought to be uncovered when assembled in the church to worship the Lord, nor that all women in all cultures, in all nations, and in all ages ought to be covered when assembled in the church to worship the Lord. For NATURE did not teach Eve to cover her head in the Garden of Eden **before the fall**, either when worshipping or not worshipping (for Adam and Eve were both naked according to Genesis 2:25, which means Eve did not wear a headcovering while in the Garden) or **after the fall** (for the Lord clothed both Adam and Eve in coats, but did not make a headcovering for Eve and place it upon her head, Genesis 3:21). NATURE certainly did not teach the priests to uncover their heads in worship in the Old Testament as a sign of male headship in the worship of God, for they were specifically commanded by God to cover their heads with a miter and bonnets (Exodus 28:4; Leviticus 8:13). Thus, once again we must not confuse the cultural and customary sign with what NATURE teaches. What NATURE teaches is NOT that a Christian man ought to be uncovered and a Christian woman ought to be covered in public worship in all churches and in all ages (or in public society at all times and in all ages). NATURE teaches that there is a distinction to be maintained between the distinctive roles and appearances between men and women. However, CULTURE specifically identifies the various outward signs and customs in which the respective roles and appearances of men and women (as taught by NATURE) are to be distinguished. We will delay a more full discussion as to what Paul means by NATURE until we address your Seventh Argument (in 1 Corinthians 11:14,15).

Third, just as Paul previously argued from the MORAL/ THEOLOGICAL principles of male headship and female submission (in 1 Corinthians 11:3) and applied it to the cultural and customary sign of male headship (i.e. the uncovered head) and the cultural and customary sign of female submission (i.e. the covered head) in 1 Corinthians 11:4-6; and just as Paul previously argued from the CREATION ORDINANCES of man being the image and glory of God, but woman being the glory of the man (in 1 Corinthians 11:7) and applied these CREATION OR-DINANCES to the cultural and customary sign of male headship (i.e. the uncovered head) in 1 Corinthians 11:7 and to the cultural and customary sign of female submission (i.e. the covered head) in 1 Corinthians 11:10; so likewise Paul now argues from PROPRIETY AND DECO-RUM asking whether it is culturally fitting and suitable for a woman to pray to God in public worship with her head uncovered in 1 Corinthians 11:13.

Fourth, as I have already mentioned in a previous letter (specifically, the first letter, dated February 4, 2011), the question that Paul asks in 1 Corinthians 11:13 ("Is it comely that a woman pray unto God uncovered?") is specifically answered by Paul after his parenthetical remarks in 1 Corinthians 11:14,15 (wherein he presents his Argument from NATURE) when he states in 1 Corinthians 11:16: "We have no such custom." In other words, when Paul states that "we have no such custom" of women praying unto God in Corinth with the cultural and customary sign of male headship (i.e. the uncovered head), he is also inferring that it WAS IN FACT a "custom" for women to pray unto God with the cultural and customary sign of female submission (i.e. the covered head). "Custom" (sunetheia) is a "habit, custom, usage" (*A Greek-English Lexicon of the New Testament*, Bauer, Arndt, and Gingrich p. 797). The only other usage of this Greek word for "custom" (sunetheia) in the Received Text of the New Testament is found in John 18:39, where it refers to the "custom" of the Jews to release one prisoner at the time of the Passover (which was obviously a national custom for the nation of the Jews and not for other nations in all ages; just as the covered head for women was a national custom among the nations and societies of the Greeks, and not a custom for all nations in all ages). In 1 Corinthians 11:16 Paul refers to the veiling of women as a "custom", which is precisely what the Reformers called it as well: a custom or customary sign. But a "custom" or "customary sign" is not the same thing as the MORAL LAW OF GOD, or the same thing as the REGULATIVE PRINCIPLE, or the same thing as a MORAL/THEOLOGICAL PRINCIPLE, or the same thing as a CREATION ORDINANCE, or the same thing as NATURE. A "customary sign" first becomes a "custom" in the society or culture at large, and is then carried over into worship when a church is planted in that cultural society, because to dismiss such a "customary sign" in worship would introduce confusion, disorder, and schism into the Church (especially when that "customary sign" is agreeable to the MORAL/THEOLOGICAL PRINCIPLE S of male headship and female submission (1 Corinthians 11:3), is agreeable to the CREATION ORDINANCE S of man being the image and glory of God and woman being the glory of man (1 Corinthians 11:9), is agreeable to PROPRIETY AND DECORUM as to what is seemly and fitting (1 Corinthians 11:13), and is agreeable to NATURE, which teaches a distinction in the respective roles and appearances of men and women (1 Corinthians 11:14). However, when in a society, nation, or culture, there is no such general or universal custom of women covering their heads when they are in public (or for men to uncover their heads when they are in public), I submit there is no sound reason for the covering of the head in the case of women and the uncovering of the head in the case of men to be practiced in the public worship of God. The Corinthians are here rebuked by Paul because the women removed the cultural and customary sign of female submission (i.e. a covered head) and appeared in public worship with the cultural and customary sign of male headship (i.e. the covered head); and in so doing they completely inverted their role and appearance as women with that of men within the cultural setting of Corinth. Instead of doing what was CULTURALLY FITTING and what was agreeable to what NATURE teaches (i.e. a distinction in the roles and appearances of men and women), the Corinthians did and tolerated what was UNFITTING, and they confused and blurred what NATURE teaches by way of gender distinctions.

Fifth, I would note, ___, that Paul is not appealing to the Corinthians "to persist in the ordinance of v. 2 (per your Sixth Argument: "6. In v. 13 he appeals to the conscience, governed by the perpetual moral law, of the Corinthians as a reason to **persist in the ordinance of v. 2**. (vs. 13)". As we have already noted in this letter, Paul is not appealing to the conscience of each individual member of the Church of Corinth (but rather to a sense of propriety and decorum among the whole Church collectively), nor is Paul looking in this case specifically to the Moral Law of God (but rather to the general principles of gender distinction taught by NATURE). And the "ordinances" of 1 Corinthians 11:2 which Paul commends the Corinthians for keeping are NEITHER the uncovered head of men

NOR the covered head of women. For if the Corinthian men were uncovered in worship, and if the Corinthian women were covered in worship (i.e. if they were faithfully keeping these practices in worship as "ordinances"), there would have been no reason at all for Paul to rebuke and correct them for NOT doing so in 1 Corinthians 11:3-16. As I previously argued, I believe these "ordinances" were left unnamed by Paul so that we are not able to specifically identify them (though no doubt the Corinthians themselves knew which apostolic "ordinances" they were keeping and those to which Paul referred).

Sixth, in conclusion and in summary, ___, I submit that Paul does not appeal to the conscience of each individual member of the Corinthian Church to follow the MORAL LAW OF GOD or the REGULATIVE PRINCIPLE OF WORSHIP in judging whether it is COMELY or FITTING for a woman to pray unto God uncovered. To the contrary, Paul commands the Corinthians to decide among themselves collectively whether it is FITTING AND SUITABLE for a woman to pray unto God uncovered as they consider that NATURE itself teaches there ought to be distinctive roles and appearances maintained between men and women.

___, please feel free to follow-up with any questions or comments you might have from my response to your Sixth Argument.

Yours for the Cause of Christ,

Greg L. Price

A Letter Responding to Argument #7 (1 Corinthians 11:14-15)

July 9, 2011

THE SEVENTH ARGUMENT FROM 1 CORINTHIANS 11:14-15

Dear ___, we come now to your Seventh Argument to support the perpetual use of headcoverings on the part of women in the public worship of God:

> 7. In vv. 14 - 15 Paul argues that nature, which teaches men to have short hair, and women long hair, demonstrates that there should be a difference in public worship (vss. 14-15) [from your email dated 1/20/11 – GLP].

___, we have previously observed from our study of headcoverings in 1 Corinthians 11 that Paul has now up to this point laid three distinct pieces of the foundation to his argument in addressing the particular abuse reported to him within the Corinthian Church. (1) The first piece of the foundation of Paul's argument is the argument from MORAL/THEOLOGICAL PRINCIPLES of headship and submission found in 1 Corinthians 11:3: "the head of the woman is the man." These MORAL/THEO-LOGICAL principles of headship and submission are then applied by Paul to the confusion and schism within the Corinthian Church in 1 Corinthians 11:4-6. (2) The second piece of the foundation of Paul's argument is the argument from CREATION ORDINANCES in 1 Corinthians 11:7: "he [i.e. man—GLP] is the image and glory of God; but the woman is the glory of the man." These CREATION ORDINANCES are further demonstrated in 1 Corinthians 11:8,9, and then are applied to the confusion and schism within the Corinthian Church in 1 Corinthians 11:7 ("For a man indeed ought not to cover his head") and in 1 Corinthians 11:10 ("For this cause ought the woman to have power on her head"). (3) The third piece of the foundation of Paul's argument is an argument from PROPRIETY AND DECORUM in 1 Corinthians 11:13 ("Judge in yourselves: is it comely that a woman pray unto God uncovered?"), which question Paul then answers (after a brief parenthesis in verses 14-15) in verse 16: "We have no such custom." This now brings us to the fourth piece of the foundation of Paul's argument against the scandal of role reversal on the part of Christian women in Corinth who were removing the cultural sign of feminine submission (the covered head) when they appeared in the public assembly of Christians in Corinth in order to worship God—an argument from NATURE as found in 1 Corinthians 11:14-15: "Doth not even nature itself teach you, that, if a man have long hair, it is a shame unto him? But if a woman have long hair, it is a glory to her: for her hair is given her for a covering."

First, though Paul now proceeds to another argument in 1 Corinthians 11:14-15, it should be noted that this argument from NATURE is yet a confirmation in Paul's inspired writing of what is NOT suitable and fitting in Corinth when it comes to a woman praying with an uncovered head in the public worship of God (1 Corinthians 11:13). In other words, the argument from NATURE (in 1 Corinthians 11:14-15) is intimately tied to the argument from PROPRIETY AND DECORUM (1 Corinthians 11:13). This close connection between 1 Corinthians 11:13 and 1 Corinthians 11:14-15 is also grammatically indicated by the Greek conjunction (in the Greek Received Text) that introduces the question asked by Paul in 1 Corinthians 11:14: "**OR** doth not even nature itself teach you, that, if a man have long hair, it is a shame unto him?" Although the translators of the Authorized Version have not translated this Greek conjunction into English, it is nevertheless the first Greek word found in the Greek text (the Received Text) and ought to be translated as "or". The conjunction, "or", clearly demonstrates the connection that exists between the argument from PROPRIETY AND DECORUM (in 1 Corinthians 11:13) and the argument from NATURE (in 1 Corinthians 11:14-15). Thus, here is another argument in 1 Corinthians 11:14-15 (that of NATURE), but one that is connected to the previous argument in 1 Corinthians 11:13 (that of PROPRIETY AND DECORUM).

Second, before considering the meaning of the word, NATURE, in the present context in which Paul uses it, it should be observed that the form of the question asked in 1 Corinthians 11:14 expects an affirmative answer of "Yes" (i.e. "Even nature itself does teach you, that, if a man have long hair, it is a shame unto him, doesn't it? Yes, it does."). For when a question is asked in the Greek language using a form of the negative, *ou*, which means "no" or "not" (the form of *ou* used here in the question in 1 Corinthians 11:14 is the Greek word, *oude*), the rhetorical question expects the response of "Yes" (cf. *A Manual of the Greek New Testament* by H. E. Dana and Julius R. Mantey, The MacMillan Company, pp. 264,265). Thus, whatever the word NATURE means here in 1 Corinthians 11:14, it should be understood at the outset that Paul expects the Christians in Corinth to agree with him that NATURE itself does indeed teach that it is a shame for a man to have long hair. That is clearly Paul's design in framing the question in the way that he does.

Third, we must now turn our attention to Paul's use of the word, NATURE, in 1 Corinthians 11:14. I think it would be most helpful to answer the following two questions in regard to the word, NATURE: (1) What is NATURE? (2) What does NATURE teach?

1. What is NATURE?

Any degree of research among commentators (both past and present) will reveal a number of varied proposals as to the meaning of NATURE intended by the Holy Spirit here in 1 Corinthians 11:14 ("Doth not even nature itself"). Among the proposals presented for the meaning of NATURE are the following (this being a representative list rather than an exhaustive list): (1) NATURE as that which is observable in God's created order; (2) NATURE as that which is a natural customary sign or practice within a society; (3) NATURE as that which comes by natural endowment; or (4) NATURE as the Light of Nature within man.

The fact that NATURE is appealed to as a teacher from which the Corinthians can learn about the proper length of hair among men and women would seem to rule out **the first option (NATURE as that which is observable in God's created order)**, for we are not told in the Genesis account how long Adam's hair was at the time that he was created. As we have already seen from Paul's second argument (in 1 Corinthians 11:7-12), which is an argument from CREATION ORDINANCES, it may be argued that NATURE as that which is revealed in the order of creation teaches that woman was created FROM man and that woman was created FOR man (and therefore, NATURE as God's created order does declare the headship of man and the submission of woman). However, it cannot be argued from NATURE (as far as what is revealed in the creation of man and woman from the Genesis account) anything specifically about the length of man's hair. Was Adam's hair shorn closely above his ears? Was Adam's head shaven of all hair? Was Adam's hair over his ears? Was Adam's hair down to his shoulders, or longer? We do not know and cannot speak with any certainty about the specific length of Adam's hair at the time of his creation. I would submit that God's created order does not actually teach the specific length of a man's hair or the specific length of a woman's hair so as to constitute what are the clear parameters of short hair for a man (so that to go beyond that length is to sin against NATURE as revealed in God's created order) and the clear parameters of long hair for a woman (so that to cut it shorter than that specific length is to sin against NATURE as revealed in God's created order). NATURE as that which is observable in God's created order does not tell us at what specific length a man's hair or a woman's hair becomes a shame to him or to her.

The second option (NATURE as that which is a natural customary sign or practice within a society) would not seem to be a use of the word, NATURE (*phusis* in Greek), that can be found anywhere in Scripture (although Calvin and others believed this to be the best proposal for the meaning of the word, NATURE, in 1 Corinthians 11:14). That would not automatically discount the possibility of such a cultural use of the word, NATURE. In fact, the immediately preceding verse (1 Corinthians 11:13) addresses that which is culturally fitting and suitable. And it should be noted that the use of the word,

NATURE (*phusis*), to refer to a natural customary sign or practice within a society is found in extra-biblical literature, even though it is not found in Scripture itself (and is not used by Paul himself elsewhere in his inspired writings). Moreover, I would also like to add that I do not deny that when specifically discussing the relative length of hair between men and women appropriate for each gender, cultural considerations will no doubt be instructive and helpful. For example, the longer hair styles that were acceptable and proper among men in the seventeenth and eighteenth centuries in Europe and America were considerably different than the shorter hairstyles that were acceptable and proper among men in the twentieth century and at least through the 1950s. I allow that such differences in the length of men's hairstyles (as well as of women's hairstyles) are a matter of cultural distinction to a very large extent (even though I do believe that NATURE ITSELF condemns a unisex hairstyle among men and women so that there is no difference in the way a man and woman look). I will have more to say about this later in my discussion. Thus, although this view of NATURE as that which is a natural customary sign or practice within a society is certainly plausible within the context of 1 Corinthians 11, the fact that neither Paul nor any other writer in the New Testament ever uses it in this sense (even though the word is used some 13 times in the New Testament), renders it less likely especially if there is another sense of the word, NATURE, that works well within the context and is used by Paul (or other New Testament writers).

The third option (NATURE as that which comes by natural endowment) likewise does not appear to be the right choice as to the meaning of NATURE in 1 Corinthians 11:14, for the relatively shorter length of a man's hair to that of the woman's (in any society) is not due so much to natural endowment, but rather to that which is really contrary to natural endowment: the barber's scissors that trim the man's hair so that it does not grow as long as the woman's hair. If Paul intended natural endowment to be the meaning of NATURE in 1 Corinthians 11:14, then the beard of a man (which naturally grows on a man's face) in distinction from the smooth face of a woman (who cannot ordinarily grow a beard) would have been a more appropriate distinction between men and women as to natural endowment.

The fourth option (NATURE as the Light of Nature within man) is in my judgment the best proposal in understanding Paul's use of the word, NATURE, in 1 Corinthians 11:14. First, Paul uses the word, NATURE, in a similar sense in Romans 2:14-15: "For when the Gentiles, which have not the law, do by **nature** the things contained in the law, these, having not the law, are a law unto themselves; which shew **the work of the law written in their hearts.**" Just as the Light of Nature instructed Gentiles who were without the written Law of God in matters of general moral principles (according to Paul in Romans 2:14-15) so as to leave them without excuse, so likewise the Light of Nature taught the Corinthians in matters of general moral principles related to distinctions between men and women. It is true that the Light of Nature within man has indeed been greatly diminished with regard to the degree of the light that is perceived in man (due to the intellectual effects of Adam's sin in all of his posterity by ordinary generation). Sinners since the fall of Adam suppress the knowledge and light of God's natural revelation that is impressed upon their reason and conscience (Romans 1:19-22). However, I submit that Paul still appeals to the Light of Nature as being a faithful teacher in regard to general moral principles of a perpetual nature that relate to proper distinctions to be maintained between men and women in 1 Corinthians 11:14. Second, the Westminster divines viewed the Light of Nature as the proper meaning of NATURE (in 1 Corinthians 11:14), for they cite among their proof texts, 1 Corinthians 11:14, as scriptural proof of the use of the Light of Nature in ordering "some circumstances concerning the worship of God, and government of the Church" that are common to human actions and societies (cf. *Westminster Confession of Faith*, 1:6). This is a significant corroborative testimony to the meaning of NATURE in 1 Corinthians 11:14, for this testimony is not only the testimony of one man, and not only the testimony of the Westminster Assembly, but is, in effect, the testimony of the three reformed kingdoms of England, Ireland, and Scotland, and their churches. Thus, I submit that the meaning of NATURE that bests explains the Spirit's intention in using the term, NATURE, is that of the Light of Nature.

2. What does NATURE teach?

Does the Light of Nature as to the general moral principles within man specifically teach what constitutes long hair on a man (whether hair over the ears, down the neck, or to the shoulders)? No, not a specific length, for the Light of Nature does not teach such specifics, but rather teaches general moral principles that are applicable to all nations and all cultures. It should be noted that the Egyptian men shaved their heads and wore no beards, while the Assyrian, Babylonian, and early Greek men wore long hair to the shoulders (if not longer) and beards as well. Later Greek and Roman men (certainly by the time that Paul penned 1 Corinthians) had turned from long hair to short hair as the new fashion in hairstyle (see *Unger's Bible Dictionary*, Merrill F. Unger, Moody Press, pp. 440-441). In fact, I would submit that one cannot even appeal to Scripture as giving a moral commandment of what specifically constitutes long hair on a man (whether hair that covers the ears, hair that covers the neck, hair that extends to the shoulders, etc.). Consider the longer hair of the Nazarite, especially those who were permanent Nazarites all their lives (and were not permitted to ever cut their hair), like Samson (Judges 13:5,7), Samuel (1 Samuel 1:11), and John the Baptist (Luke 1:15). The longer hair of the Nazarite was, in fact, a sign of his consecration to the Lord (according to Numbers 6:5-8). Moreover, it would appear that Absalom was noted and praised in all Israel for his masculine beauty and his longer hair, which he trimmed only once a year (according to 2 Samuel 14:25-26). The bride describes the hair of her beloved husband in this way: "his locks are bushy" or as the marginal note in the Authorized Version states, "curled" (Song of Solomon 5:11). The Hebrew word translated "locks" in Song of Solomon 5:1 (as in the seven "locks" of Samson's head in Judges 16:19) would certainly seem not to be the short hairstyle of men in the 1950s. Josephus describes Solomon's body guard as consisting of men of youthful beauty and having "luxuriant heads of hair" (*Antiquities*, VIII, vii, 3 [185]). In fact, God strictly forbade the cutting of the hair of men around the corners (or sides) of the head due to its conformity to idolatrous nations (in Leviticus 19:27; Jeremiah 9:26 [see the marginal note in the Authorized Version]; Jeremiah 25:23 [see the marginal note in the Authorized Version]; Jeremiah 49:32 [see marginal note in the Authorized Version].Thus, I believe we must forego any such moral specifications as to what precisely constitutes long hair on a man (whether a shaved head, a shorn hairstyle, hair over the ears, hair down the neck, hair to the shoulders, etc.) in seeking to understand what NATURE teaches, for I cannot find in the Light of Nature or in the Light of Scripture any such moral precision as to the specific length of a man's hair (and at what length a man's hair specifically becomes a sin). Does that then make Paul's words meaningless? Absolutely not!

In light of the fact that God in His Word did not universally condemn what many in our present age may consider to be long (or longer) hair on a man, how are we to understand Paul's words in 1 Corinthians 11:14? Does Paul actually mean that the Light of Nature itself PRECISELY STATES and DECLARES as an explicit moral commandment that which many at this present time would consider long hair on a man (e.g. shoulder-length hair) and that which is a shame to him? If so, we would then also expect that the Light of Nature would tell us what precisely constitutes long hair on a man so that he doesn't sin by bringing shame upon himself. But the Light of Nature does not provide that kind of precise information, nor does the Light of Scripture do so (as I have also noted above). What then does Paul mean when he states, "Doth not even nature itself teach you, that, if a man have long hair, it is a shame unto him?" In the very next verse (1 Corinthians 11:15), Paul uses the same Greek word for "long hair" (*koma*), but uses it in reference to a woman's "long hair". In other words, I would submit that Paul appeals to NATURE (i.e. the Light of Nature implanted by God within each person) as teaching that a man's hairstyle and a woman's hairstyle ought to be distinguishable one from the other. A man's hair as to its length should not be longer than the general custom of a woman's hair in that society. If a man's hairstyle (or length) looks like that of a woman's (or for that matter, if a woman's hairstyle or length looks like that of a man's) so that there is a unisex hairstyle in appearance and length, then one has violated what NATURE (i.e. the Light of Nature within each person) universally teaches by way of the distinction that ought to exist in the roles and appearances of men and women. This distinction

114

between men and women is also taught in a passage like the following: "The woman shall not wear that which pertaineth unto a man, neither shall a man put on a woman's garment: for all that do so are abomination unto the LORD thy God" Deuteronomy 22:5). In other words, just as cross-dressing is an abomination in confusing, rather than distinguishing, a man and a woman, so cross-hairstyling is a shame to a man (and to a woman) in confusing, rather than distinguishing, a man and a woman.

Thus, NATURE (i.e. the Light of Nature) provides the Corinthians with GENERAL moral principles, not with SPECIFIC moral commandments as to precise definitions of hair length. And the GENERAL moral principle that is revealed by the Light of Nature about men and women is that men and women are to be distinguishable in their respective roles of male headship and female submission, and in their respective appearances in appearance. However, it is the respective cultures that will speak more specifically to the precise length of hair that is appropriate to men and women, respectively.

Fourth, it should once again be noted that Paul's argument from NATURE does not merely apply to worship. In other words, hairstyles of men and women (and the respective lengths of their hair) are not limited to when men and women only gather for the public worship of God. NATURE speaks to all men and women in society (Christian and non-Christian alike) whether they are gathered for worship or whether they are purchasing produce at the local market. Thus, one cannot build an argument from NATURE for the use of headcoverings and apply it to the public worship of God alone (which is the domain of the Regulative Principle of Worship), for NATURE transcends ecclesiastical society and worship to include civil society and assemblies as well. Those who would limit Paul's argument to only the ecclesiastical assembly would have to conclude that NATURE (i.e. the Light of Nature) is only operative in Christians (as opposed to non-Christians) and only operative in Christians when they gather for public worship (as opposed to when they are walking from one shop to another). I would submit that just as Paul takes MORAL/THEOLOGICAL PRINCIPLES (in 1 Corinthians 11:3) and applies them to a cultural issue in the Church of Corinth (i.e. the uncovered head of men and the covered head of women), and just as he takes CREATION ORDINANCES (in 1 Corinthians 11:7) and applies them to a cultural issue in the Church of Corinth (i.e. the uncovered head of men and the covered head of women), so he takes NATURE (i.e. the Light of Nature) and applies it to a cultural issue in the Church of Corinth (i.e. the uncovered head of men and the covered head of women).

Fifth, Paul now gives a contrast in regard to "long hair", distinguishing "long hair" on a woman from "long hair" on a man. Long hair on a woman is not a shame (as it is for a man), but is rather a "glory" to her (i.e. it is a feminine adornment of beauty unique to her, just as the priestly garments were uniquely a glory and beauty to them, according to Exodus 28:40). Paul then concludes this fourth piece of the foundation of his argument (from NATURE) against the public scandal of role reversal on the part of Christian women in Corinth who were removing the cultural sign of feminine submission (the covered head) when they appeared in the public assembly of Christians in Corinth. Paul concludes this argument from NATURE (i.e. the Light of Nature) by giving a reason for the feminine glory and beauty of "long hair": "for her hair is given her for a covering" (1 Corinthians 11:15). As already noted above, Paul uses the same Greek word here in 1 Corinthians 11:15 when speaking of a woman's hair (*koma*), as was used previously when speaking of a man's hair in 1 Corinthians 11:14. In both cases, the reference is not merely to hair, but to "long hair." Paul in effect concludes, "A woman is given her long hair for the following reason: because NATURE (i.e. the Light of Nature) teaches her that her "long hair" is given to her for (or "as") a natural veil indicating her feminine submission to male headship. Let us be clear here. The Light of Nature speaks to the subject of the respective and distinctive roles and hairstyles appropriate to men and women, whereas the Corinthian culture speaks to the subject of fabric headcoverings. Paul draws out a parallel between the Light of Nature in regard to hair and the Corinthian culture as to fabric headcoverings. In Corinth (unlike many contemporary nations and cultures where women are not covered in public), such a parallel might be used by Paul between the long hair of a woman as a natural veil of submission consistent with the Light of Nature and between the fabric headcovering of a woman as a cultural sign of submission. In Corinth, where a woman wore a fabric headcovering in civil society and ecclesiastical society, Paul could reason very convincingly that just as Corinthian culture gave a woman a fabric headcovering, so Nature (i.e. the Light of Nature) has given her a natural headcovering. And even though modern Western culture has not given a woman a fabric headcovering to wear in civil society and ecclesiastical society, NATURE (i.e. the Light of Nature) has still given to a woman (particularly to a Christian woman) a natural headcovering in her hair that should indicate her submission to men. The style of her hair and the length of her hair should not confuse her with a man. Let the natural glory and beauty of the long hair of a Christian woman (at least longer than that of men in general within any given culture or society) testify that she is taught by NATURE (i.e. the Light of Nature) to find her God-given role in submitting to male headship.

Sixth, I agree with you, ___, when you state that Paul's argument from NATURE "demonstrates that there should be a difference in public worship." Yes, because NATURE (i.e. the Light of Nature) teaches that men and women are to be distinguished one from the other in their respective roles of male headship and female submission, and in their respective appearances relating to hairstyles, these gender distinctions taught by the Light of Nature ought also to be manifested in whatever cultural customs that distinguish men from women in civil society (like the uncovered head of a man and the covered head of a woman, or gender segregated seating, etc.). And these cultural customs in civil society (like the uncovered head of a man and the covered head of a woman, or gender segregated seating, etc.) that mirror the Light of Nature in regard to the respective and distinctive roles and appearances of men and women ought as well to be carried over into ecclesiastical society when the church gathers to worship the Lord. In the cultural context of Corinth, the uncovered head of a man and the covered head of a woman in civil society did in fact reflect the Light of Nature (just as gender segregated seating did at that time as well), therefore, Paul argues that the Corinthians ought to learn from NATURE itself (which teaches respective and distinctive roles and appearances of men and women) that it is not fitting or suitable for a woman to pray unto God in public worship with her head uncovered (NOT because the uncovered head of a man and the covered head of a woman were specifically taught by the Light of Nature, but because the cultural custom in Corinth of the uncovered head of a man and the cultural custom in Corinth of the covered head of a woman reflected the general moral principle taught in the Light of Nature, namely, that there are respective and distinctive

118

roles and appearances appropriate for men vs. women).

Dear ___, I will pause here for any comments or questions you might have on this my Response to your Seventh Argument for the perpetual use of headcovering for women in the public worship of God.

As always, thank you for this opportunity.

Yours for the Cause of Christ,

Greg L. Price

A Letter Responding to Argument #8 (1 Corinthians 11:16)

July 18, 2011

THE EIGHTH ARGUMENT FROM 1 CORINTHIANS 11:16

Dear ___, we finally arrive at your Eighth (and final) Argument to support the perpetual use of headcoverings on the part of women in the public worship of God:

> 8. In v. 16 it appears that Paul for the second time appeals to Apostolic tradition so that should anyone challenge his argument they are 'contentious'. I would ask, how could someone ever cease to practice head-covering and not be labeled 'contentious'? (vs. 16) [from your email dated 1/20/11 – GLP].

We have covered a lot of ground in studying Paul's inspired words concerning headcoverings in 1 Corinthians 11. And yet I pray it has been a profitable study for us all.

By way of summary, as we approach Paul's last argument in 1 Corinthians 11:16, let us do a quick review of his previous arguments leading up to his final argument. ___, we have previously observed from our study of headcoverings in 1 Corinthians 11 that Paul has now up

to this point laid four distinct pieces of the foundation to
his argument in addressing the particular abuse reported
to him within the Corinthian Church. (1) The first piece
of the foundation of Paul's argument is the argument
from MORAL/THEOLOGICAL PRINCIPLES of headship and submission found in 1 Corinthians 11:3: "the
head of the woman is the man." These MORAL/THEO-
LOGICAL principles of headship and submission are
then applied by Paul to the confusion and schism within
the Corinthian Church in 1 Corinthians 11:4-6. (2) The
second piece of the foundation of Paul's argument is the
argument from CREATION ORDINANCES in
1 Corinthians 11:7: "he [i.e. man—GLP] is the image and
glory of God; but the woman is the glory of the man."
These CREATION ORDINANCES are further demonstrated in 1 Corinthians 11:8,9, and then are applied to
the confusion and schism within the Corinthian Church
in 1 Corinthians 11:7 ("For a man indeed ought not to
cover his head") and in 1 Corinthians 11:10 ("For this
cause ought the woman to have power on her head").
(3) The third piece of the foundation of Paul's argument
is an argument from PROPRIETY AND DECORUM in 1
Corinthians 11:13 ("Judge in yourselves: is it comely that
a woman pray unto God uncovered?"), which question
Paul then answers (after a brief parenthesis in verses 14-
15) in verse 16: "We have no such custom." (4) The fourth
piece of the foundation of Paul's argument against the
scandal of role reversal on the part of Christian women
in Corinth who were removing the cultural sign of
feminine submission (the covered head) when they appeared in the public assembly of Christians in Corinth
in order to worship God is an argument from NATURE
(i.e. the Light of Nature) as found in 1 Corinthians 11:14-
15: "Doth not even nature itself teach you, that, if a man
have long hair, it is a shame unto him? But if a woman
have long hair, it is a glory to her: for her hair is given

121

her for a covering." We now come to Paul's fifth and final piece of the foundation of Paul's argument against the public scandal raised in the Corinthian Church by women who were removing the cultural and customary sign of female submission when they gathered for the public worship of God: an argument from ECCLESIASTICAL UNIFORMITY ("But if any man seem to be contentious, we have no such custom, neither the churches of God" 1 Corinthians 11:16).

First, Paul begins his final argument in 1 Corinthians 11:16 with an adversative conjunction ("but", *de* in Greek) to counter any yet remaining opposition from the Corinthians. It's as if Paul stated, "I have presented a number of convincing arguments in what I have already said that should settle the scandal that has divided the Church of Corinth, BUT for those who choose to continue to dispute this matter and divide the church over it, I now appeal to my final argument."

Second, after the adversative conjunction ("but"), Paul introduces his final argument with a conditional "if" sentence (i.e. a sentence beginning with the Greek word, *ei*), which is a conditional sentence of reality (i.e. a conditional sentence which Paul assumes to be true and consistent with what is really the case, at least among a number of those in the Church of Corinth). If we were to bring out the full force of this conditional sentence of reality, we would understand Paul to be saying at this point: "But IF any one seems to disagree with me and to be contentious as to the scandal involved over a woman praying in the public worship of God in the customary sign of male headship (i.e. an uncovered head) after all that I have argued, AND I ASSUME THAT SOME WILL YET BE CONTENTIOUS OVER THIS MATTER IN THE CHURCH OF CORINTH . . ." Thus, Paul actually anticipates further contention by some within the Church of Corinth.

Third, the consequence of the conditional "if" sentence stated by Paul then follows: "we have no such custom, neither the churches of God." In other words, if (as Paul anticipates) there are those in the Church of Corinth that still seem to be divisive after what he has already stated, THEN those contentious individuals must finally face the consequence that they are entirely alone in their view, for neither the apostles nor the churches of Christ agree with such a custom as a woman praying in the public assembly with her head uncovered. In this statement is displayed an argument from ECCLESIASTICAL UNI-FORMITY (where the "we" of the apostles is combined with the "churches of God") to demonstrate that even in the matter of "custom" that is brought into the church from outside the church, ECCLESIASTICAL UNIFOR-MITY is a very important consideration; whether it be the uncovered head as a customary sign of headship and the covered head as a customary sign of submission; or foot washing as a customary sign of loving service; or kissing as a customary sign of friendly greeting; or bowing as a customary sign of subjection; or gender segregated seating as a customary sign of distinction between men and women, etc.). Such customary signs that clearly pertain to the cultures and nations into which the Gospel of Jesus Christ comes have a place in the public worship of God when the customary signs are in agreement with MOR-AL/THEOLOGICAL PRINCIPLES, CREATION ORDI-NANCES, PROPRIETY AND DECORUM, NATURE, and ECCLESIASTICAL UNIFORMITY.

Fourth, I submit that the accurate translation of the Greek adjective, *toiauten*, is "such", "we have no SUCH custom" (as is translated in the *Authorized Version*,

Young's Literal Translation of the Holy Bible, The New King James Version) and not "other" (as is translated in *The New International Version*, or *New American Standard Bible*). For as standard Greek lexicons indicate, *toiauten* clearly mean "such" rather than "other": *A Greek Lexicon of the New Testament and Other Early Christian Literature* by Bauer, Arndt, and Gingrich, The University of Chicago Press, pp. 828,829; *Greek-English Lexicon* by Liddell and Scott, Oxford University Press, p.708; *Manual Greek Lexicon of the New Testament* by Smith, University Press Aberdeen, p.447; *Greek-English Lexicon of the New Testament* by Thayer, Broadman Press, p.627). It is most important that we maintain the accurate translation of the words used in the Greek text in order to be faithful interpreters of God's Holy Word, but in this specific case, only the word "such" clarifies what Paul means within the context. For Paul had asked a question in 1 Corinthians 11:13 ("Is it comely that a woman pray unto God uncovered?"), and after his parenthetical argument from NATURE in 1 Corinthians 11:14-15, the question he had asked in 1 Corinthians 11:13 is given an answer in 1 Corinthians 11:16: "we have no SUCH custom, neither the churches of God." If Paul had meant to say, "We have no OTHER custom", it would have appeared that Paul was contradicting all that he had previously said by now saying, "we have no OTHER custom than for a woman to pray with her head uncovered." Clearly, Paul did not contradict what he had previously said. Thus, the accurate translation of the Greek adjective, *toiauten*, is "such" ("we have no SUCH custom").

Fifth, we move on now to consider the noun ("custom") which the adjective ("such") modifies. Paul declares, "we have no such CUSTOM" (where the Greek noun, *sunetheia*, is used). The Greek noun, *sunetheia*, means a "habit, custom, usage" (according to *A Greek Lexicon of the New*

Testament and Other Early Christian Literature by Bauer, Arndt, and Gingrich, The University of Chicago Press, p. 797); a "use, custom, habit, usage" (according to *Greek-English Lexicon* by Liddell and Scott, Oxford University Press, p. 676); a "habit, custom" (according to *Manual Greek Lexicon of the New Testament* by Smith, University Press Aberdeen, p. 429); and a "custom" (according to *Greek-English Lexicon of the New Testament* by Thayer, Broadman Press, p. 604). Paul infers that the use of a headcovering by women in the public worship of God was not determined by the Regulative Principle of Worship, but was rather a custom that was brought into worship from the general practice of women in society wearing a headcovering in the cultural context of Corinth. For if Paul declares that there is no such "custom" for women to pray in public worship without a covered head, then Paul also infers that it was a received "custom" for women to pray with a covered head in worship. The only other usage of this Greek word for "custom" (*sunetheia*) in the Received Text of the New Testament is found in John 18:39, where it refers to the "custom" of the Jews to release one prisoner at the time of the Passover (which was obviously a national custom for the nation of the Jews alone and not for all nations throughout time, just as the covered head for women was a national custom among the nations and societies of the Greeks and not for all nations throughout time). Here Paul refers (by inference) to the veiling of women as a "custom", which is precisely what the Reformers called it as well: a custom or customary sign. But a "custom" or "customary sign" is not the same thing as a scripturally regulated act or practice of worship. A "customary sign" first becomes a "custom" in the society or culture at large, and is then carried over into worship when a church is planted in that cultural society because to dismiss such a "customary sign" in worship would introduce confusion, disorder, and schism into the Church (especially when that "customary sign" is agreeable to MORAL/THEOLOGICAL PRINCIPLES, CREATION ORDINANCES, PROPRIETY AND DECORUM, NATURE, and ECCLESIASTICAL UNIFORMITY). However, when in a society, nation, or culture, there is no such general or universal custom of women covering their heads when they are in public (or for men to uncover their heads when they are in public), I submit there is no sound reason for the covering of the head in the case of women or the uncovering of the head in the case of men to be used in the public worship of God (per Paul's requirement). The Corinthians are here rebuked by Paul because the women removed the customary sign of female submission (i.e. a covered head) when they appeared in public worship, thus completely inverting their respective role as outwardly indicated by the customary sign of that general society within Corinth. No other Divine "ordinance" in Scripture is ever referred to as a mere "custom" or "habit" (*sunetheia*). Thus, I submit that Paul distinguishes the veiling of women (as a "custom" within Greek society at large) in 1 Corinthians 11:16 from the regulated Divine "ordinances" or apostolic "traditions" referred to in 1 Corinthians 11:2,23.

Sixth, I submit, therefore, that the "custom" referred to in 1 Corinthians 11:16 ("We have no such custom") does NOT refer to some alleged "custom" of being contentious; for being contentious is not a mere "custom", but is rather a divisive and scandalous sin in all cultures and in all ages. The Greek word used for "contentious" is *philoneikos* (which literally means "a love of strife"). However, the Corinthians had begun practicing and tolerating within their assemblies a pernicious and scandalous "custom" of women being uncovered as they prayed jointly with other Christians in the public worship of God. It is far more reasonable and agreeable to the context of 1 Corinthians 11 to understand the "custom" here addressed by Paul to be a practice that deals with outward adornment and decorum (which is the thrust of Paul's remarks in 1 Corinthians 11) than for the "custom" to be an express moral evil. The following commentators seem to me to handle the text at this point most accurately.

A. R. FAUSSET (*A Commentary Critical, Experimental, and Practical on the Old and New Testaments,* William B. Eerdmans Publishing Co., 1 Corinthians, Vol. 3, p. 315)

> **no such custom** — as that of women praying uncovered. Not 'that of being contentious.' The Greek (*sunetheian* [custom — GLP]) implies *usage* rather than *a mental habit* (John 18:39) [1 Corinthians 11:16 — GLP].

FREDERIC LOUIS GODET (*Commentary on First Corinthians,* Kregel Publications, pp. 559,560)

> The love of disputation is a fault, a bad habit, but not a custom. To call the habit of discussion an ecclesiastical usage! No. The only custom of which there can be any question here is that on which the whole passage has turned: women speaking without being veiled.

CHARLES HODGE (*A Commentary on 1 & 2 Corinthians,* Still Waters Revival Books, p. 214)

> Calvin, and many of the best modern com-

mentators, give a different view of this passage. They understand the apostle to say, that if any one seems to be disputatious, neither we nor the churches are accustomed to dispute. It is not our wont to waste words with those who wish merely to make contention. The only reason assigned for this interpretation, is Paul's saying *we have* no such custom; which they say cannot mean the custom of women going unveiled. But why not? The apostles and the churches constituted a whole—neither the one nor the other, neither the churches nor their infallible guides, sanctioned the usage in question. Besides, no other custom is mentioned in the context than the one which he has been discussing. "*If* any one appear contentious," is not a custom and suggests nothing to which the words *such a custom* can naturally refer.

G. G. FINDLAY (*The Expositor's Greek Testament*, William B. Eerdmans Publishing Company, 1 Corinthians, p. 876)

[T]he custom described in vv. 4 f. above, which gave rise to the whole discussion; not, as many understand it, *the custom of being contentious* (a *temper*, surely, rather than a custom).

HENRY ALFORD (Alford's Greek Testament—An Exegetical and Critical Commentary, Guardian Press, 1 Corinthians, p. 569)

But surely it would be very unlikely, that after *so long a treatment of a particular subject*, the Apostle should wind up all by merely a censure of a fault *common* to their behavior on *this and all the other* matters of dispute. Such a rendering seems to me almost to *stultify the conclusion*: 'If any will dispute about it still, remember that it is neither our practice, nor that of the Churches, *to dispute.*' It would seem to me, but for the weighty names on the other side, hardly to admit of a question, that the *sunetheia* [custom—GLP] alludes to *the practice* (see ref. John [18:39—GLP]) *of women praying uncovered.*

GORDON D. FEE (*The New International Commentary on the New Testament,* William B. Eerdmans Publishing Company, 1 Corinthians, pp. 529,530)

The opening sentence, "If anyone wants to be contentious about this," is one of four such sentences in this letter, each indicating that this is what some are doing. Most likely this refers to some women who are discarding a traditional "covering" of some kind. Paul's final appeal to these women is that "we have no such practice [custom—GLP]—nor do the churches of God." The words "such practice [custom—GLP]," therefore, must refer to that which the "contentious" are advocating, and which this argument has been combating.

129

Seventh, Paul's argument in 1 Corinthians 11:16 is an argument from ECCLESIASTICAL UNIFORMITY ("we have no such custom, neither the churches of God."). ECCLESIASTICAL UNIFORMITY is so foreign to contemporary churches because such an argument strikes at the worldly principles of independence, autonomy, diversity, pluralism, and multiformity upon which contemporary churches so much thrive. But biblical unity within the Church of Jesus Christ is not only a mystical and spiritual unity, but is also a unity that is to manifest itself in ECCLESIASTICAL UNIFORMITY (at least to the nearest degree possible). Consider the ECCLESIASTICAL UNIFORMITY of the Old Testament (Exodus 12:48-49; Numbers 18:5; Joshua 22:11-29; 1 Kings 12:26-33) and of the New Testament (1 Corinthians 4:17; 1 Corinthians 14:33). The "oneness" that is ours spiritually in Christ is to be evidenced in a visible unity in "one" doctrine, "one" worship, "one" church government, and "one" church discipline (John 17:20-21; Ephesians 4:1-6; 1 Corinthians 1:10). This biblical principle was the stated purpose and end of *The Solemn League and Covenant* (1643) that bound the Kingdoms and Churches of Scotland, England, and Ireland (and all their posterity):

> I. That we shall sincerely, really, and constantly, through the grace of GOD, endeavour, in our several places and callings, the preservation of the reformed religion in the Church of Scotland, in doctrine, worship, discipline, and government, against our common enemies; the reformation of religion in the kingdoms of England and Ireland, in doctrine, worship, discipline, and government, according to the word of GOD, and the example of the best reformed Churches; and shall endeavour to bring the

Churches of GOD in the three kingdoms to the nearest conjunction and uniformity in religion, confession of faith, form of church-government, directory for worship and catechising; that we, and our posterity after us, may, as brethren, live in faith and love, and the Lord may delight to dwell in the midst of us.

In fact, it was *The Solemn League and Covenant* that was the first document approved by the Westminster Assembly and that was intended to be the covenantal basis for uniformity among the three Kingdoms and Churches of Scotland, England, and Ireland (and all their posterity) in approving all of the other documents (*The Confession of Faith, The Directory for the Public Worship of God, The Presbyterial Form of Church Government, The Larger Catechism,* and *The Shorter Catechism*). In the title page of each of these documents approved by the Westminster Assembly, one will find the following notation:

Agreed upon by the Assembly of Divines at Westminster, with the assistance of commissioners from the Church of Scotland, AS A PART OF THE COVENANTED UNIFORMITY IN RELIGION BETWIXT THE CHURCHES OF CHRIST IN THE KINGDOMS OF SCOTLAND, ENGLAND, AND IRELAND.

What Paul was teaching by way of ECCLESIASTICAL UNIFORMITY (even in matters related to cultural customs among those who had the same cultural customs) is perfectly consistent with what was decided by the Synod that met in Jerusalem (Acts 15). There the apostles and elders of the churches met together to resolve matters

131

related not only to moral issues (like justification by faith alone, and fornication), but also to certain Jewish practices carried over from the Old Testament into the New Testament age that were not intended to be perpetually binding for all ages to come (such as circumcision, eating meat offered to idols, meat that was strangled, or blood). The differences between Jewish Christians and Gentile Christians on some of these issues (that were neither related to the Moral Law of God or to the Regulative Principle of Worship in the New Covenant) were causing schisms, divisions, and scandal within the churches of Christ. Thus, in order to promote biblical unity among the churches of Christ at that time, the apostles and elders decided what were the matters that must be avoided (whether of a moral nature or of a customary nature) in order to promote unity and uniformity among the churches of Christ. This is precisely Paul's line of argument in 1 Corinthians 11:16 when he implicitly appeals to the uniformity of a cultural "custom" followed at that time by the apostles and the churches of God. The fact that Paul addresses a cultural custom in 1 Corinthians 11 and implicitly appeals to the apostles and the churches of God by way of ECCLESIASTICAL UNIFORMITY does not make the cultural custom of the headcovering any more universal for all churches in all ages than the use of ECCLESIASTICAL UNIFORMITY in Acts 15:20 regarding meat that is strangled makes that judicial law universal for all churches in all ages. For ECCLESIASTICAL UNIFORMITY may apply not only to matters that are doctrinal, but to matters that are cultural as well (when the peace, purity, and unity of the church are threatened).

Eighth, ___ I would therefore have to disagree with you when you indicate that 1 Corinthians 11:16 is an appeal to "apostolic tradition": "In v. 16 it appears that Paul for the second time appeals to Apostolic tradition." I do agree that Paul refers to apostolic tradition when he mentions "ordinances" in 1 Corinthians 11:2 (you might want to review what was said in the first letter concerning the use of the word "ordinances"). However, I disagree that Paul refers to apostolic tradition when he mentions the word "custom" in 1 Corinthians 11:16. As already noted, a cultural "custom" is not apostolic tradition or revelation given by Christ to His Church. A cultural "custom" is that which is practiced by society in general and may be brought into worship when it is agreeable to MORAL/THEOLOGICAL PRINCIPLES, CREATION ORDINANCES, PROPRIETY AND DECORUM, NATURE, and ECCLESIASTICAL UNIFORMITY, and when to disregard that cultural custom would bring division, disorder, and confusion into the Church of Christ. Paul's appeal is NOT to apostolic tradition, but is rather an appeal to ECCLESIASTICAL UNIFORMITY in regard to the cultural custom of men being uncovered and women being covered in the public worship of God within the Church of Corinth.

Ninth, ___ you ask, "how could someone ever cease to practice headcovering and not be labeled 'contentious'? " I respond, the same question might be asked with regard to a host of other cultural customs that prevailed in ancient times, such as washing the feet of the saints, greeting the saints with a holy kiss, gender segregated seating etc. If any group of Christians in the churches at the time of the apostles refused to honor the cultural practices mentioned above, there would no doubt result division and disorder within the Christian congregations, and Paul would have addressed these resulting scandals in the same way that he addressed the scandal associated with headcoverings. Those who might refuse to follow the cultural custom of greeting one another with a holy kiss (and might prefer to shake hands instead) would likewise be addressed as "contentious" by Paul, for they would be disregarding established customs that were at least agreeable to MORAL/THEOLOGICAL PRINCIPLES, PROPRIETY AND DECORUM, and ECCLESIASTICAL UNIFORMITY. Since greeting one another with a holy kiss is commanded on a number of occasions by Paul (Romans 16:16; 1 Corinthians 16:20; 2 Corinthians 13:12; 1 Thessalonians 5:26), I might ask, "How could someone ever cease to practice greeting one another with a holy kiss and not be labeled 'contentious'?" In that cultural context, one could not cease to do so without being contentious. However, in a cultural context in which greeting one another with a holy kiss is not a custom in society at large, then it would not be contentious for a group of Christians to shake hands with one another rather than giving a holy kiss. So it is likewise the case with the cultural custom of the covered head of a female and the cultural custom of the uncovered head of a male. In the cultural context of Corinth, where the covered head of a woman in general society was a sign of feminine submission, a woman could not remove her head-covering when she gathered to worship the Lord without being contentious. However, in a cultural context in which the covered head of a woman in general society is not a customary sign of female submission, then it would not be contentious for a woman to join in the public worship of God with her head uncovered.

____, this concludes my Response to your Eighth Argument. Please send me any follow-up questions you might have from my Response, or any comments that you believe would be helpful. Having completed my Responses to all of your Arguments, I would like to conclude my correspondence on this matter by collating the words of a number of writers, commentators, and divines who corroborate the position that Paul viewed the matter of

headcoverings in
1 Corinthians 11 as being a cultural custom or customary practice rather than a practice regulated by the Moral
Law of God or the Regulative Principle of Worship.
Thanks again, ___.

Yours for the Cause of Christ,

Greg L. Price

A Letter Presenting Some Historical Testimony Which Corroborates the Customary View of Headcoverings

August 1, 2011

Headcoverings — A Brief Representation of Historical Testimony

The following citations are not intended to be exhaustive, but representative of a number of scholars, divines, and commentators that indicate that Paul's instruction concerning the practice of women covering the head in public worship and the practice of men uncovering the head in public worship (in 1 Corinthians 11) was not founded upon some specification in the Moral Law of God or required by the Regulative Principle of Worship, but was founded upon a cultural, customary sign that was carried over into the public worship of God (and therefore temporary and alterable among nations, cultures, and times) in order to preserve the peace, purity, and unity of Christ's Church in the Corinthian's context. Emphases in each citation are indicated by highlighting in bold, and older forms of spelling have been changed to conform to contemporary standards.

JOHN CALVIN (*Men, Women and Order in the Church,* Presbyterian Heritage Publications, pp. 24,60)

Let us observe that St. Paul has only taken exception to something that was not appropriate and fitting **according to the usage of the land**. For (as we have shown) **we are not to take those countries and measure them by our custom(s)** [1 Corinthians 11:4 — GLP].

Now, if this rule [found in 1 Corinthians 11:16 — GLP] must be observed in **small things** [Calvin considers the headcovering to be a "small thing" and hardly "of any importance" rather than a moral commandment based upon the Regulative Principle of Worship — GLP], **which hardly seem to be of any importance**, how about when it comes to doctrine? St. Paul says that if we find **an accepted custom** in a people — in a church — then we must conform; each one may not do his own thing: rather we must demonstrate our desire to nurture peace [1 Corinthians 11:16 — GLP].

JOHN CALVIN (*Institutes of the Christian Religion,* The Westminster Press, Vol. 2, pp. 1207,1208)

There are examples of the first sort in Paul: that profane drinking bouts should not be mingled with the sacred supper of the Lord (1 Cor. 11:21-22), **and that women should not go out in public with uncovered heads (1 Cor. 11:5)**. And we have many others in daily use, such as: that we pray with knees bent and **head bare** . . .

But because he [God—GLP] did not will in outward discipline and ceremonies to prescribe in detail what we ought to do **(because he foresaw that this depended upon the state of the times, and he did not deem one form suitable for all ages)**, here we must take refuge in those general rules which he has given, that whatever the necessity of the church will require for order and decorum should be tested against these. Lastly, because he [God—GLP] has taught nothing specifically, and because these things are not necessary to salvation, **and for the upbuilding of the church ought to be variously accommodated to the customs of each nation and age, it will be fitting (as the advantage of the church will require) to change and abrogate traditional practices and to establish new ones** [Calvin looks back to that which he said in the previous pages (p. 1206,1207) as to what Paul taught in regard to proper decorum in Corinth, namely, that it was not proper decorum for women to go out in public society with uncovered heads (not just ecclesiastical assemblies or public worship, but public society in general, which indicates Calvin believed the covered head of a woman in Corinth was NOT a regulated aspect of worship); and he also looks back to the previous page (p. 1207) as to what he said was proper decorum for all in Geneva (not just men, but men and women) who prayed, namely, to do so with "knees bent" and with "head bare". Calvin says that all such matters of decorum "ought to be variously accommodated to **the customs of each nation and age**" —GLP].

THEODORE BEZA (*King James Bible with Geneva Bible Notes* on 1 Corinthians 11, Still Waters Revival Books, p. 156)

> It appeareth, that this was a politic law **serving only for the circumstances of the time that Paul lived in,** by this reason, **because in these our days for a man to speak bare-headed in an assembly, is a sign of subjection** [1 Corinthians 11:4—GLP].

JOHN DIODATI (*Pious and Learned Annotations upon the Holy Bible* on 1 Corinthians 11, Still Waters Revival Books)

> A new precept, or renewed by the Apostle concerning public civility, in habit; namely, that women in public assemblies of the Church should be covered, and men should have their heads uncovered, **by reason that in those places and times the covered head was [a—GLP] sign of subjection, and an uncovered [head—GLP] contrariwise a mark of liberty and command**: wherefore that they might keep in the Church that degree among sexes which God had established[,] they were to observe such signs and marks thereof **as were used by the**

common consent of Nations [1 Corinthians 11:3 – GLP].

DUTCH ANNOTATIONS UPON THE BIBLE (1 Corinthians 11, Still Waters Revival Books)

[verse 4 – GLP] he dishonors his own head (namely, forasmuch as the uncovering of the head was **then** a sign of power and dominion, as on the contrary **now at this day** those that have power over others, will keep their heads covered, and they that are under others will uncover their heads before them. But in all these things, **we must always have respect to the use of divers times and countries**, and what is honorable and edifying therein, 1 Cor. 14:40; Phil. 4:8).

WILLIAM AMES (*A Fresh Suit Against Human Ceremonies*, Still Waters Revival Books, pp. 345)

Concerning Women's Veils, 1 Cor. 11.

[T]he veil was neither apostolical, nor merely of human institution, nor of instituted signification, nor yet appropriated unto God's worship: **but a civil order of decency, used as well out of God's worship as in it**. And the Rejoinder [i.e. Dr. Burgess, not to be confused with either Anthony Burgess or Cornelius Burgess – GLP] granteth, that **it was a civil custom**.

SAMUEL RUTHERFORD (*The Divine Right of Church Government and Excommunication*, Still Waters Revival Books, pp. 89,90)

The learned Salmasius thinketh it [i.e. the uncovering of the head — GLP] but **a national sign of honor, no ways universally received** . . . The Jews to this day, as of old, used not uncovering the head as a sign of honor: But by the contrary, covering was a sign of honor. If therefore the Jews, being made a visible Church, shall receive the Lord's Supper, and pray and prophesy with covered heads, men would judge it no dishonoring of their head, or not of disrespect of the Ordinances of God. Though Paul having regard to **a national custom**, did so esteem it.

DAVID DICKSON (*Commentary on the Epistles*, 1 Corinthians 11)

[1 CORINTHIANS — GLP] CHAP. XI.

THE SEVENTH ARTICLE CONCERNING ORDER AND DECENCY.

Vers. 13. *Judge in you selves, is it comely that a woman pray unto God uncovered?*
14. *Doth not even nature it self teach you, that if a man have long hair, it is a shame unto him?*
15. *But if a woman have long hair, it is a glory to her; for her hair is given her for a covering.*

Argum. 8. Common sense, and nature itself,

or natural inclination **(so he calls settled custom, and agreeable to nature, in respect to what is comely) dictates that it is unseemly for a woman to pray uncovered,** or that a man should wear long hair, and the contrary is decent: Therefore you observe no decorum when you behave yourselves otherwise.

Vers. 16. *But if any man seem to be contentious, we have no such custom, neither the Churches of God.*

Argum. 9. If any perhaps should not be moved by these Arguments, but should contend, the Apostle opposeth to their contentious Apologies, **the received and established custom of the Jews,** and the rest of the Churches: Other Churches have no such custom, that women should be present at public assemblies, with their heads uncovered, and the man with his head covered: Therefore your custom not agreeing with decency, either according to natural use, or of the Churches, is altogether unseemly.

GEORGE GILLESPIE (*A Dispute Against English Popish Ceremonies*, Naphtali Press, pp. 247,248)

There are three sorts of signs here to be distinguished. 1. Natural signs: so smoke is a sign of fire, and the dawning of the day a sign of the rising of the sun. 2. **Customable signs; and so the uncovering of the head, which of old was a sign of preeminence,**

has, through custom, become a sign of subjection. 3. Voluntary signs, which are called *signa instituta* [*instituted signs*]; these are either sacred or civil. **To appoint sacred signs of heavenly mysteries or spiritual graces is God's own peculiar [prerogative], and of this kind are the holy sacraments.** Civil signs for civil and moral uses may be, and are, commendably appointed by men, both in church and commonwealth; and thus the tolling of a bell is a sign given for assembling, and has the same signification both in ecclesiastical and secular assemblings. . . . Secondly, **customary signs** have likewise place in divine service; for so a man coming into one of our churches in time of public worship, if he see the hearers covered [apparently both men and women were covered in the Scottish worship service, contrary to what Paul states in 1 Corinthians 11 where a distinction is to be made between the covering of women and the non-covering of men — GLP], he knows by this **customary sign** that sermon has begun.

JAMES DURHAM (*Concerning Scandal*, Naphtali Press, p. 20)

Assertion Two. Yet in other things [i.e. in things that are not necessary duties--GLP] there ought to be great respect had to offense, and men ought to be swayed accordingly in their practice, as the former reasons clear. As (1), **if the matter is of light con-**

cernment in itself, as how men's gestures are in their walking (suppose in walking softly, or quickly, with cloak or without) men ought to do, or abstain, as may prevent the construction of pride, lightness, etc., or give occasion to others in any of these. Of such sort are salutations in the very manner of them. **Of this sort was womens' praying with their heads uncovered amongst the Corinthians,** it being **then** taken for an evil sign [Durham notes that the uncovered head of a woman in public worship was "of light concernment in itself" and not a necessary duty (i.e. required by the Moral Law or Regulative Principle of Worship), and he also notes that "then", at Paul's time, the uncovered head of a woman in public worship was "taken for an evil sign; which implies that it is no longer the case in Durham's time — GLP].

FRANCIS TURRETIN (*Institutes of Elenctic Theology*, P&R Publishing, Vol. 2, p. 95)

Although certain ordinations of the apostles (which referred to the rites and circumstances of divine worship) were **variable and instituted only for a time** (as the sanction concerning the not eating of blood and of things strangled [Acts 15:20]; **concerning the woman's head being covered and the man's being uncovered when they prophesy [1 Cor. 11:4,5]**) because there was a special cause and reason for them and (this ceasing) the institution itself ought to

cease also; still there were others invariable and of perpetual observance in the church, none of which were founded upon any special occasion to last only for a time by which they might be rendered temporary (such as the imposition of hands in the setting apart of ministers and the distinction between the offices of deacon and pastor).

MATTHEW POOLE (*Matthew Poole's Commentary on the Holy Bible*, MacDonald Publishing Company, 1 Corinthians, pp. 576,577)

His argument seemeth to be this, That the woman in religious services ought to behave herself as a person in subjection to her husband, and accordingly to use such a gesture, as, **according to the guise and custom of that country**, testified such a subjection [1 Corinthians 11:3 – GLP].

Interpreters rightly agree, that **this and the following verses are to be interpreted from the customs of countries**; and all that can be concluded from this verse is, that it is the duty of men employed in Divine ministrations, to look to behave themselves as those who are to represent the Lord Jesus Christ, behaving themselves with a just authority and gravity that becometh his ambassadors, **which decent gravity is to be judged from the common opinion and account of the country wherein they live**. . . but the apostle's arguing from the man's headship , seemeth to import that the reason of this assertion of the apostle was, **be-cause in Corinth the uncovered head was a sigh of authority**. At this day the Maho-metans (or Turks) speak to their superiors covered, and so are covered also in their re-ligious performances. **The custom with us in these western parts is quite otherwise; the uncovering of the head is a sign or token of subjection:** hence ministers pray and preach with their heads uncovered, to denote their subjection to God and Christ; **but yet this custom is not uniform, for in France the Reformed ministers preach with their heads covered; as they pray un-covered, to express their reverence and subjection to God so they preach covered, as representing Christ, the great Teacher from whom they derive, and whom they represent.** Nothing in this is a further rule to Christians, than that it is the duty of min-isters, in praying and preaching, to use pos-tures and habits that are not naturally, **nor according to the custom of the place where they live**, uncomely and irreverent, and so looked upon [1 Corinthians 11:4 — GLP].

[I]t being **in those places** accounted an immodest thing for a woman to appear in public uncovered [1 Corinthians 11:5 — GLP].

SIMON BROWNE (*Matthew Henry's Commentary*, Mac-Donald Publishing Company, 1 Corinthians, p. 561)

The thing he reprehends is the woman's praying or prophesying uncovered, or the man's doing either covered v. 4,5. To understand this, it must be observed that it was a signification either of shame or subjection for persons to be veiled, or covered, **in the eastern countries, contrary to the custom of ours, where the being bareheaded betokens subjection, and being covered superiority and dominion** [1 Corinthians 11:4,5 — GLP].

JOHN BROWN OF HADDINGTON (*The New Self-Interpreting Bible library*, Still Waters Revival Books, 1 Corinthians, p. 360)

Now the veiling of the head being a badge of modesty and subjection, and uncovering of it a token of superiority, **in your country and many others**, every man, who, by an extraordinary influence of the Spirit, leads your public worship in praying or preaching with a veil on his head or face, dishonors Jesus Christ, from whom he received his authority [1 Corinthians 11:4 — GLP].

If therefore women will throw off their veils, those badges of modesty and subjection, let them cut their hair short as men do: and if, as everyone must, **they think that immodest and contrary to custom, let them keep on their veils** [1 Corinthians 11:6 — GLP].

CHARLES HODGE (*A Commentary on 1 & 2 Corinthians,* Still Water Revival Books, pp. 204,205)

[1 CORINTHIANS – GLP] CHAPTER XI

On the impropriety of women appearing in public unveiled, Vs. 2-16.

HAVING corrected the more private abuses which prevailed among the Corinthians, the apostle begins in this chapter to consider those which relate to the mode of conducting public worship. The first of these is the habit of women appearing in public without a veil. **Dress is in a great degree conventional. A costume which is proper in one country, would be indecorous in another. The principle insisted upon in this paragraph is, that women should conform in matters of dress to all those usages which the public sentiment of the community in which they live demands. The veil in all eastern countries was, and to a great extent still is, the symbol of modesty and subjection. For a woman, therefore, in Corinth to discard the veil was to renounce her claim to modesty, and to refuse to recognize her subordination to her husband. It is on the assumption of this significancy in the use of the veil, that the apostle's whole argument in this paragraph is founded.**

A. R. FAUSSET (*A Commentary Critical, Experimental, and*

Practical on the Old and New Testaments, William B. Eerdmans Publishing Company, 1 Corinthians, Vol. 3, pp. 313,314)

The Corinthians women, on the ground of the abolition of distinction of sex in Christ, claimed equality with men, and, overstepping propriety, came forward to pray and prophesy **without the customary headcovering** {1 Corinthians 11:3 — GLP].

The Greek custom was for men in worship to be uncovered; the Jews wore the Tallith, or veil, to show reverence and their sense of unworthiness in God's presence (Isa. vi.2), **excepting where (as in Corinth) the Greek custom prevailed** [1 Corinthians 11:4 — GLP].

A. T. ROBERTSON (*Word Pictures in the New Testament,* Broadman Press, Vol. 5, p. 160,161,162)

It is public praying and prophesying that the Apostle here has in mind. He does not here condemn the act, **but the breach of custom which would bring reproach** [1 Corinthians 11:5 — GLP].

He reinforces the appeal to custom by the appeal to nature in a question that expects the affirmative answer (*oude*) [1 Corinthians 11:14 — GLP].

F. W. GROSHEIDE (*The New International Commentary on the New Testament,* William B. Eerdmans Publishing Company, 1 Corinthians, p. 253)

> But everybody will understand that it must have been very objectionable for a woman to speak in public with her head unveiled **in a country where custom dictated that honorable women wore a veil or a fillet in public** [1 Corinthians 11:4 — GLP].

GORDON D. FEE (*The New International Commentary on the New Testament,* William B. Eerdmans Publishing Company 1 Corinthians, p. 530)

> **The very 'customary' nature of the problem,** which could be argued in this way in a basically monolithic cultural environment, makes it nearly impossible to transfer 'across the board' to the multifaceted cultures in which the church finds itself today — even if we knew exactly what it was we were to transfer, which we do not. **But in each culture there are surely those modes of dress that are appropriate and those that are not** [1 Corinthians 11:16 — GLP].

www.ingramcontent.com/pod-product-compliance
Lightning Source LLC
Chambersburg PA
CBHW051042030426
42339CB00006B/152